Modern Soccer Tactics & Strategy

Insights into the Modern Game: Formations, Positions, Styles & Systems

Dan Jones

PREFACE

Whether you're a passionate player, an aspiring coach, or just someone who loves the beautiful game, this book is for you.

Over the last few decades, soccer (as we'll call it in this book) tactics have undergone a fascinating evolution. Gone are the days of rigid 4-4-2 formations and kick-and-rush tactics. The modern game demands a more sophisticated, fluid, and adaptable approach on the pitch.

In this book, we'll look into the cutting-edge tactics and strategies that are shaping the way soccer is played today. From the false nine to the gegenpressing system, from the inverted winger to the ball-playing center-back, we'll explore the innovative thinking that has revolutionized the sport.

But tactics are more than just formations and buzzwords. They're about understanding the roles and responsibilities of each position, the patterns of play in attack and defense, and the balance between risk and reward. We'll break it all down for you, position by position, phase by phase.

You'll learn how the world's best teams like Barcelona, Bayern Munich, and Manchester City have mastered the art of possession play, how to create overloads and exploit defensive weaknesses, and how to transition seamlessly from attack to defense (and back again).

We'll also explore the growing influence of technology in tactical planning, from data analytics to video analysis tools, and how these innovations are giving teams an unprecedented edge.

Whether you're a seasoned pro or just starting your soccer journey, this book will provide you with a deep understanding of the modern game's tactical nuances. It's not just about memorizing formations or replicating strategies – it's about developing a tactical mindset that will help you read the game, anticipate movements, and make split-second decisions on the pitch.

So lace up your boots, grab a pen and paper, and get ready to dive into modern soccer tactics and strategy. The game has never been more exciting, and with this book as your guide, you'll be ready to take your understanding (and your game) to the next level.

TOPICAL OUTLINE

Introduction to Modern Soccer Tactics
- Evolution of Soccer Tactics
- Overview of Modern Tactical Trends

Chapter 1: Position-Specific Tactical Roles and Responsibilities
- Goalkeepers
- Central Defenders
- Fullbacks (Left Back and Right Back)
- Defensive Midfielders
- Central Midfielders
- Wing Players
- Attacking Midfielders
- Strikers

Chapter 2: Formations and Their Evolution
- Classic Formations: 4-4-2, 3-5-2
- Modern Adaptations: 4-3-3, 4-2-3-1
- Innovative Setups: 3-4-3, 3-4-2-1

Chapter 3: Attacking Play in Modern Soccer
- Building from the Back
- Patterns of Play in the Final Third
- Use of Overloads and Underloads
- False Nines and Their Influence
- Inside Forwards vs. Traditional Wingers
- Role of the Target Man

Chapter 4: Defending in the Modern Game
- High Pressing Systems
- Compact Defending
- Role of Defenders in Initiating Attacks
- High Line vs. Deep Line
- Use of Sweeper Keepers
- Defensive Compactness

Chapter 5: Modern Midfield Play
- Role of the Deep-Lying Playmaker
- Box-to-Box Midfielders
- Creative Midfielders

Chapter 6: Balanced Play: Finding the Right Mix

- Transitioning between Attack and Defense
- Maintaining Shape
- Balancing Risk and Reward

Chapter 7: Counterattacks

- Speed and Precision
- Triggers for Counterattacks
- Role of Transition Players

Chapter 8: High Press: Putting Opponents Under Pressure

- Triggers for the Press
- Coordinated Pressing Movements
- Risks and Rewards

Chapter 9: Wing Play in the Modern Game

- Importance of Width
- Overlapping Fullbacks
- Inverted Wingers
- Why Wing Play Is Less Relevant in Modern Soccer

Chapter 10: Role of Fullbacks in the Modern Game

- Evolution from Defenders to Attackers
- Defensive Duties
- Contribution to Attack

Chapter 11: Possession Play

- Maintaining Possession
- Building Through the Thirds
- Importance of Ball Retention

Chapter 12: Transition Play

- Offensive Transitions
- Defensive Transitions
- Role of Key Players

Chapter 13: Passing Styles

- Short Passing vs. Long Passing
- Importance of Passing Lanes
- Passing Under Pressure
- Passing as Communication

Chapter 14: Creating Space

- Movement Off the Ball
- Exploiting Defensive Weaknesses
- Use of Decoys

Chapter 15: Exploiting Weaknesses
- Analyzing Opponents
- Targeting Specific Players or Areas
- Adjusting Tactics Accordingly

Chapter 16: Set Pieces and Dead Ball Situations
- Free Kicks: Direct vs. Indirect
- Corners and Throw-Ins
- Penalty Strategies

Chapter 17: Technology in Tactical Planning
- Use of Data Analytics
- Video Analysis Tools
- GPS and Wearable Technology

Chapter 18: Changing Tactics During a Game
- Recognizing the Need for Change
- Making Effective Substitutions
- Tactical Adjustments

Chapter 19: Opponent Analysis and Scouting
- Pre-Match Analysis
- How to Choose Tactics Based on Opponent
- In-Game Observations
- Post-Match Review

Chapter 20: Tactical Periodization
- Planning the Season
- Balancing Training Loads
- Tactical Drills and Exercises

Chapter 21: Man Marking vs. Zonal Marking
- Principles of Man Marking
- Advantages and Disadvantages of Zonal Marking
- Hybrid Systems

Chapter 22: Player Movements and Rotations
- Rotational Play in Midfield
- Positional Interchange in Attack

- Defenders Joining the Attack

Chapter 23: Effective Use of Substitutions and In-Game Changes
- Timing of Substitutions
- Tactical Shifts

Chapter 24: Tactics for Weaker Teams vs. Tactics for Stronger Teams
- Strategies for Underdogs
- Approaches for Dominant Teams

Chapter 25: Game Management Tactics
- Playing from Different Scorelines (Winning, Losing, Drawing)
- Tactical Adjustments Based on Score
- Protecting a Lead vs. Chasing a Game
- Use of Time-Wasting Tactics
- Mentality and Motivation in Different Game States

Chapter 26: Tactical Lessons from the World's Best Clubs
- Case Studies: Barcelona, Bayern Munich, Manchester City
- Learning from Success
- Adapting Strategies

Appendix

Afterword

TABLE OF CONTENTS

INTRODUCTION TO MODERN SOCCER TACTICS

Evolution of Soccer Tactics

Soccer tactics have evolved dramatically over the years, reflecting changes in the game's rules, player skillsets, and the constant quest for a competitive edge.

The Early Days: Simplicity and Directness

In the early days of soccer, tactics were simple and direct. The 2-3-5 formation, known as the "pyramid," dominated the game. This formation emphasized attacking play, with five forwards leading the charge. However, it lacked defensive solidity, often leaving teams vulnerable to counterattacks.

The Rise of WM and the Italian Catenaccio

In the 1930s, Herbert Chapman introduced the WM formation, a revolutionary system that focused on both attack and defense. This formation saw the midfielders drop deeper to support the defense, creating a more balanced approach. The WM formation paved the way for the Italian "catenaccio" system, a highly defensive tactic that prioritized organization and discipline. The catenaccio system became synonymous with Italian football in the 1960s, leading to numerous successes in both domestic and international competitions.

Total Football and the Dutch Revolution

In the 1970s, Dutch football introduced the concept of "Total Football." This innovative system emphasized fluidity, interchangeability, and constant movement. Players were encouraged to switch positions seamlessly, creating a dynamic and unpredictable style of play. Total Football revolutionized the game, inspiring a generation of coaches and players.

The Rise of Possession Football and Tiki-Taka

In the late 20th century, possession football emerged as a dominant tactic. Teams like Barcelona and Spain popularized the "tiki-taka" style, characterized by short, intricate passing and high pressing. This approach aimed to control the game's tempo and create scoring opportunities through patient build-up play. Tiki-taka's success led to a global resurgence in possession-based tactics.

The Gegenpressing Era and High-Intensity Football

The 21st century saw the rise of "gegenpressing," a high-intensity pressing tactic popularized by Jurgen Klopp's Borussia Dortmund and Liverpool teams. Gegenpressing involves immediately pressing the opposition after losing possession, aiming to win the ball back quickly and launch rapid counterattacks. This aggressive style demands immense physical fitness and tactical discipline but can be devastatingly effective when executed properly.

Overview of Modern Tactical Trends

Modern soccer tactics are a fascinating blend of innovation and adaptation. As the sport evolves, so do the strategies employed on the pitch. Let's explore some key trends shaping the tactical landscape of modern soccer:

Positional Play and Fluidity: Teams are moving away from rigid formations and embracing fluidity. Positional play, championed by coaches like Pep Guardiola, emphasizes players occupying specific zones on the field to create passing triangles and maintain control of the game. This approach demands high levels of spatial awareness and intelligent movement.

High Pressing and Counter-Pressing: Teams are becoming more aggressive in their defensive approach, employing high pressing to win the ball back quickly in the opponent's half. Counter-pressing, which involves immediate pressure after losing possession, aims to disrupt the opposition's counterattack before it gains momentum.

Inverted Fullbacks: Traditionally defensive players, fullbacks are now increasingly involved in the build-up play. Inverted fullbacks tuck into midfield, creating numerical superiority in central areas and offering an additional passing option. This tactic can overload the opposition's midfield and create opportunities for through balls or switches of play.

False Nines: The traditional center-forward role is evolving. False nines are strikers who drop deep into midfield, dragging defenders out of position and creating space for attacking midfielders to exploit. This tactic can confuse the opposition's defensive structure and open up new avenues for attack.

High Defensive Lines: Teams are pushing their defensive lines higher up the field, compressing the playing space and limiting the time and space available to the opposition. This aggressive approach requires excellent coordination and communication among defenders but can be highly effective in suffocating the opposition's attack.

Set-Piece Specialization: Set pieces, such as free kicks and corners, are increasingly seen as valuable scoring opportunities. Teams are investing significant time and resources into developing specialized routines and training players to execute them with precision.

Data-Driven Analysis: The use of data analytics is transforming the way teams prepare for matches. Coaches are using data to gain insights into opponents' weaknesses, identify areas for improvement in their team's performance, and develop tailored game plans. This data-driven approach is revolutionizing tactical decision-making in modern soccer.

Understanding these trends is essential for anyone who wants to deepen their knowledge and appreciation of soccer tactics.

CHAPTER 1: POSITION-SPECIFIC TACTICAL ROLES AND RESPONSIBILITIES

Goalkeepers

In modern soccer, the goalkeeper is not merely a last line of defense; they are the foundation upon which a team's attacking play is built. The demands placed on goalkeepers have expanded significantly, requiring a diverse skill set that goes beyond shot-stopping.

Shot-Stopping and Reflexes: This remains a fundamental requirement. Goalkeepers must possess excellent reflexes, agility, and positioning to deny the opposition from scoring. Modern goalkeepers are expected to make acrobatic saves, command their penalty area, and deal decisively with crosses and set-pieces.

Distribution and Playmaking: The modern goalkeeper is the first attacker. They initiate build-up play from the back, either through short, accurate passes to defenders or long, precise balls to midfielders and forwards. Goalkeepers must be comfortable with the ball at their feet and possess excellent passing range and accuracy. This ability to launch attacks quickly and effectively can catch opponents off guard and create scoring opportunities.

Sweeper-Keeper: The goalkeeper's role extends beyond the penalty area. Modern goalkeepers act as sweeper-keepers, anticipating danger and rushing off their line to intercept through balls, clear loose balls, and act as an extra defender. This requires exceptional reading of the game, speed, and decision-making skills.

Communication and Leadership: Goalkeepers are the eyes and ears of the team. They must organize the defense, communicate instructions to their teammates, and maintain a calm demeanor under pressure. Effective communication is crucial for ensuring defensive solidity and preventing misunderstandings that could lead to goals.

Tactical Awareness: Goalkeepers must understand the tactical nuances of the game. They need to read the opposition's attacking patterns, anticipate their movements, and adjust their positioning accordingly. This involves studying opponents before matches, analyzing their strengths and weaknesses, and adapting their approach to neutralize the threat.

Adaptability: The modern game demands versatility from goalkeepers. They must be able to adapt to different playing styles, whether it's a possession-based approach that requires building from the back or a counter-attacking style that demands quick distribution and long-range passing.

Physical and Mental Strength: Goalkeeping is physically demanding, requiring agility, strength, and endurance. Goalkeepers must also be mentally resilient, able to cope with the pressure of high-stakes situations and bounce back from mistakes.

Examples of Modern Goalkeepers: Some prime examples of modern goalkeepers who excel in these diverse roles include:

- **Manuel Neuer (Bayern Munich/Germany):** A pioneer of the sweeper-keeper role, known for his exceptional distribution and commanding presence.
- **Alisson Becker (Liverpool/Brazil):** A master shot-stopper with impeccable positioning and a calming influence on his defense.
- **Ederson Moraes (Manchester City/Brazil):** Renowned for his distribution and passing range, often initiating attacks from the back.
- **Marc-André ter Stegen (Barcelona/Germany):** A skilled sweeper-keeper with a penchant for making crucial saves and starting attacks from deep.

These goalkeepers have redefined the position, showcasing the diverse skill set required to thrive in the modern game. They are not just shot-stoppers but playmakers, leaders, and tactical lynchpins for their teams.

Pay attention to the goalkeeper's role. Observe how they contribute to both defensive and attacking phases of play. Analyze their decision-making, communication, and technical skills.

Central Defenders

Central defenders are the bedrock of a team's defensive structure, tasked with thwarting opposition attacks and initiating offensive moves. Their role has evolved significantly, demanding a diverse skill set that combines physicality, technical ability, and tactical intelligence.

Defensive Responsibilities: Central defenders must excel at the core aspects of defending. This includes winning aerial duels, making well-timed tackles and interceptions, tracking runs, and anticipating opponents' movements. They must be comfortable defending one-on-one situations and organizing the defensive line to maintain a compact shape and deny space for attackers.

Man-Marking and Zonal Marking: Central defenders must be proficient in both man-marking and zonal marking systems. Man-marking involves closely tracking a specific opponent, while zonal marking focuses on defending specific areas of the pitch. Modern defenders often switch between these approaches based on the game situation and the strengths and weaknesses of the opposition attackers.

Build-up Play and Distribution: The modern central defender is not just a destroyer; they are also a creator. They are fundamental in initiating attacks from the back, either through short, accurate passes to midfielders or long, diagonal balls to wingers. This requires composure on the ball, excellent passing range, and the ability to break lines with penetrative passes.

Leadership and Communication: Central defenders are often the vocal leaders of the defense. They must organize the defensive line, communicate instructions to their teammates, and maintain a calm demeanor under pressure. Effective communication is vital for ensuring defensive solidity and preventing misunderstandings that could lead to goals.

Tactical Versatility: Central defenders must be adaptable and able to adjust to different tactical systems. This includes playing in a back four, a back three, or even as part of a hybrid system. They must also be able to adapt to different defensive approaches, such as high pressing or a deeper defensive block.

Aerial Threat: Central defenders are expected to be a threat in both boxes. They must be able to win aerial duels in their own penalty area to clear crosses and set-pieces. They should also pose an aerial threat in the opposition's box during attacking set-pieces, potentially scoring crucial goals.

Examples of Modern Central Defenders: Some prime examples of modern central defenders who excel in these diverse roles include:

- **Virgil van Dijk (Liverpool/Netherlands):** A dominant aerial presence with exceptional defensive positioning and the ability to launch attacks from deep.
- **Sergio Ramos (Paris Saint-Germain/Spain):** A vocal leader with a fierce competitive spirit, known for his tackling ability and goal-scoring prowess.
- **Kalidou Koulibaly (Chelsea/Senegal):** A powerful and athletic defender with excellent pace and the ability to carry the ball out of defense.
- **Ruben Dias (Manchester City/Portugal):** A tactically astute defender with exceptional reading of the game and composure on the ball.
- **Leonardo Bonucci (Juventus/Italy):** A master of defensive positioning and organization, known for his accurate passing and leadership qualities.

These defenders represent the epitome of the modern central defender, showcasing the diverse skill set required to thrive in the contemporary game. They are not just defenders but playmakers, leaders, and tactical assets for their teams.

Fullbacks (Left Back and Right Back)

The fullback position has undergone a radical transformation in modern soccer, evolving from primarily defensive stalwarts to dynamic contributors in both attack and defense. Let's break down the key roles and responsibilities of left backs (LB) and right backs (RB) in the contemporary game:

Defensive Responsibilities:

- **Containing Wingers:** Fullbacks are the first line of defense against opposition wingers. They must track their runs, deny them space, and prevent crosses into the box. This requires speed, agility, and a keen understanding of defensive positioning.
- **Winning One-on-One Duels:** Fullbacks often face tricky wingers who excel at dribbling and creating chances. They must be able to win one-on-one duels through well-timed tackles, interceptions, and physicality.
- **Tracking Overlapping Runs:** As modern fullbacks push forward, they must also be aware of overlapping runs from their own wingers. This requires constant communication and coordination to ensure the defensive line remains compact and organized.
- **Aerial Defending:** Fullbacks must be competent in aerial duels, both in defending crosses and winning headers in their own box during set-pieces.

Attacking Responsibilities:

- **Overlapping Runs:** Fullbacks make surging runs down the flanks, providing width and creating numerical overloads in attacking areas. This requires stamina, pace, and the ability to time their runs effectively.
- **Delivering Crosses:** Fullbacks are expected to deliver accurate crosses into the box, creating scoring opportunities for their teammates. This requires good crossing technique and an understanding of where to place the ball to maximize the chances of a goal.
- **Cutting Inside:** Inverted fullbacks often cut inside from their flank, drifting into central areas to create passing options and contribute to the build-up play. This requires good dribbling skills and the vision to pick out passes.
- **Creating Chances:** Fullbacks can be creative outlets for their team, providing through balls, cutbacks, and even scoring goals themselves. This requires good technical ability and an attacking mindset.

Tactical Versatility:

- **Adapting to Different Systems:** Fullbacks must be adaptable to different formations and systems, whether it's a back four, a back three, or even a wing-back role in a 3-5-2 formation. They must be comfortable playing both high and wide or as inverted fullbacks, depending on the team's tactical approach.
- **Switching Play:** Fullbacks are critical in switching the point of attack, using their passing range to quickly move the ball from one flank to the other. This can create opportunities to exploit space on the opposite side of the field.
- **Pressing High:** In teams that employ a high-pressing style, fullbacks are expected to push up and press the opposition high up the pitch. This requires excellent fitness levels and the ability to quickly transition between attacking and defending.

Examples of Modern Fullbacks:

- **Trent Alexander-Arnold (Liverpool/England):** A creative force from right back, known for his exceptional crossing ability and playmaking skills.
- **Andrew Robertson (Liverpool/Scotland):** A tireless left back with incredible stamina, overlapping runs, and pinpoint deliveries into the box.
- **João Cancelo (Manchester City/Portugal):** A versatile fullback capable of playing on either flank, known for his technical ability, dribbling skills, and attacking prowess.
- **Achraf Hakimi (Paris Saint-Germain/Morocco):** A dynamic right back with blistering pace and an eye for goal, often making marauding runs forward.

Defensive Midfielders

The defensive midfielder (DM) is the unsung hero, the linchpin that holds the team's tactical structure together. Their role is multifaceted, demanding a blend of defensive grit, tactical acumen, and playmaking ability. Let's look into the key responsibilities of this crucial position.

Shielding the Defense: The DM is the first line of defense in front of the backline. Their primary task is to protect the central defensive area, preventing opponents from penetrating through the middle. They achieve this by intercepting passes, tackling opponents, and disrupting the opposition's build-up play. This requires excellent positional awareness, anticipation, and a strong tackling technique.

Regaining Possession: DMs are often the first to press the opposition when possession is lost. They must be aggressive in their approach, harrying opponents and forcing them into mistakes. Their ability to win back the ball quickly is crucial for launching counterattacks or maintaining control of the game.

Distribution and Circulation: Once possession is regained, the DM is responsible for distributing the ball effectively. This can involve short, simple passes to maintain possession or longer, more ambitious passes to initiate attacks. They must be comfortable on the ball and possess excellent passing range and accuracy.

Tactical Awareness: DMs must have a high level of tactical understanding. They need to read the game, anticipate opponents' movements, and adjust their positioning accordingly. This involves identifying passing lanes, anticipating potential threats, and communicating instructions to their teammates.

Controlling the Tempo: DMs are critical in controlling the tempo of the game. They can slow down the pace by keeping possession and recycling the ball, or they can accelerate the game by playing forward passes and initiating quick attacks. Their ability to dictate the rhythm of the match is invaluable for their team.

Leadership and Communication: DMs are often the vocal leaders on the pitch, organizing the midfield and defense. They must communicate effectively with their teammates, providing instructions and encouragement. Their leadership qualities are essential for maintaining team cohesion and morale.

Versatility: The modern DM is not just a defensive specialist. They must also be capable of contributing to the attack. This can involve making forward runs, joining the attack in the final third, and even scoring goals. Their versatility adds another dimension to the team's play.

Different Types of DMs: There are different types of DMs, each with their own unique strengths and weaknesses. Some DMs are primarily defensive-minded, focusing on shielding the defense and breaking up play. Others are more creative, known for their passing ability and vision. And some are a combination of both, capable of fulfilling both defensive and attacking responsibilities.

Examples of Modern DMs: Some prime examples of modern DMs who excel in these diverse roles include:

* **Casemiro (Manchester United/Brazil):** A tenacious defensive midfielder known for his tackling ability, physicality, and aerial dominance.
* **Rodri (Manchester City/Spain):** A composed and intelligent midfielder with excellent passing range and the ability to dictate the tempo of the game.
* **Joshua Kimmich (Bayern Munich/Germany):** A versatile midfielder who can play as a DM or a right back, known for his defensive work rate, attacking contributions, and leadership qualities.

- **Fabinho (Liverpool/Brazil):** A complete defensive midfielder with exceptional positional awareness, tackling ability, and passing skills.
- **Declan Rice (Arsenal/England):** A young and dynamic midfielder with a high work rate, strong tackling, and the ability to drive forward with the ball.

These DMs are the epitome of the modern defensive midfielder, showcasing the diverse skill set required to thrive in the contemporary game. They are not just ball winners but playmakers, leaders, and tactical lynchpins for their teams.

Central Midfielders

Central midfielders are the heartbeat of the team, orchestrating the rhythm of play and influencing both defensive and attacking phases. Their role is multifaceted, demanding a blend of technical skill, tactical awareness, and physical endurance. Let's look into the key responsibilities of this pivotal position:

Linking Defense and Attack: Central midfielders act as the bridge between the defensive and attacking units. They receive the ball from defenders, initiate build-up play, and transition the team into the attacking phase. Their ability to link play effectively is crucial for maintaining possession, creating scoring opportunities, and controlling the flow of the game.

Dictating Tempo and Rhythm: Central midfielders are responsible for setting the tempo and rhythm of the match. They can slow down the pace by keeping possession and recycling the ball, or they can inject urgency by playing forward passes and driving into the attacking third. Their ability to dictate the tempo can significantly impact the game's outcome.

Creativity and Vision: Central midfielders must possess creativity and vision to unlock defenses. They can create chances through incisive passes, through balls, or clever dribbles. Their ability to see and exploit space is essential for breaking down organized defenses and unlocking tight matches.

Defensive Contributions: Central midfielders are not just playmakers; they also contribute significantly to the defensive effort. They must track back to support the defense, intercept passes, and make tackles. Their work rate and defensive discipline are crucial for maintaining a balanced team structure.

Transitions: Central midfielders are very important in transitions, both from defense to attack and vice versa. They must be able to quickly react to changes in possession, either by pressing the opposition or initiating counterattacks. Their adaptability and decision-making in these transitional moments can be game-changing.

Shooting and Goal Scoring: While their primary role is not to score goals, central midfielders can contribute significantly to the team's attacking output. They often arrive late in the box to unleash shots from distance or capitalize on rebounds. Their ability to score goals adds another dimension to their game and makes them more unpredictable for opponents.

Leadership and Communication: Central midfielders are often the vocal leaders on the pitch, organizing the team's shape and communicating instructions to their teammates. Their leadership qualities are essential for maintaining team cohesion and morale.

Different Types of Central Midfielders:

- **Box-to-Box Midfielder:** These players are all-rounders, contributing to both attack and defense with their tireless running, tackling ability, and passing range.
- **Deep-Lying Playmaker (Regista):** These players sit deeper in midfield, orchestrating the build-up play with their vision and passing accuracy.
- **Attacking Midfielder (Trequartista):** These players operate in the space between the midfield and attack, creating chances with their dribbling, passing, and shooting abilities.
- **Mezzala:** These midfielders play on the half-spaces, drifting wide or inside depending on the situation. They possess a blend of creative and defensive qualities.

Examples of Modern Central Midfielders:

- **Kevin De Bruyne (Manchester City/Belgium):** A creative force with exceptional vision, passing range, and goal-scoring ability.
- **Luka Modric (Real Madrid/Croatia):** A master of controlling the tempo of the game, known for his dribbling, passing, and tactical intelligence.
- **N'Golo Kante (Chelsea/France):** A tireless ball-winner with incredible stamina, tackling ability, and positional awareness.
- **Frenkie de Jong (Barcelona/Netherlands):** A composed and technically gifted midfielder with excellent ball control, passing, and dribbling skills.
- **Nicolo Barella (Inter Milan/Italy):** A dynamic box-to-box midfielder with a high work rate, strong tackling, and the ability to create and score goals.

These are just a few examples of the diverse range of central midfielders in the modern game. Each player brings their unique skill set and style to the position, making it one of the most exciting and unpredictable roles in soccer.

Wing Players

Wing players, whether they are traditional wingers or modern inside forwards, are the creative sparks that ignite a team's attacking play. Their roles have evolved significantly in modern soccer, demanding a blend of technical skill, tactical awareness, and explosive athleticism. Let's look into the key responsibilities of these dynamic players.

Width and Stretching the Defense: Wing players provide important width to a team's attacking shape. By hugging the touchline, they stretch the opposition's defense horizontally, creating space in central areas for their teammates to exploit. This stretching of the defense opens up passing lanes, creates opportunities for crosses, and forces defenders to make difficult decisions.

Dribbling and Beating Opponents: Wing players are often tasked with taking on defenders in one-on-one situations. They must possess excellent dribbling skills, close ball control, and the ability to change direction quickly. Their ability to beat opponents creates numerical superiority in attacking areas, leading to scoring opportunities.

Crossing and Delivery: Wing players are expected to deliver accurate crosses into the box. This requires excellent technique, timing, and the ability to judge the movement of their teammates. They must be able to whip in dangerous crosses from wide areas or cut inside to deliver pinpoint passes.

Cutting Inside and Shooting: Modern wing players often cut inside from the flanks, drifting into central areas to create shooting opportunities. This requires good dribbling skills, the vision to find space, and a powerful shot. Their ability to cut inside and score goals adds another dimension to their attacking threat.

Tracking Back and Defensive Contributions: Wing players are not just attacking threats; they also have defensive responsibilities. They must track back to support their fullbacks, help defend against opposition counterattacks, and win back possession. Their defensive work rate and discipline are crucial for maintaining a balanced team structure.

Combinations and Link-Up Play: Wing players often combine with fullbacks, central midfielders, and strikers to create intricate attacking moves. They must be able to quickly exchange passes, create triangles, and overload specific areas of the pitch. Their ability to link up with teammates is essential for breaking down organized defenses.

Different Types of Wing Players:

- **Traditional Winger:** These players primarily operate on the flanks, hugging the touchline and looking to deliver crosses into the box.
- **Inverted Winger:** These players prefer to cut inside from the flank onto their stronger foot, creating shooting opportunities or playing incisive passes.
- **Inside Forward:** These players operate in the half-spaces between the wing and the center of the pitch. They combine with midfielders and strikers, creating chances through dribbling, passing, and movement.

Examples of Modern Wing Players:

- **Mohamed Salah (Liverpool/Egypt):** A prolific goal-scorer with exceptional dribbling skills, pace, and a deadly finishing ability.
- **Neymar Jr. (Paris Saint-Germain/Brazil):** A creative and flamboyant winger known for his dribbling wizardry, flair, and ability to create and score goals.
- **Sadio Mané (Bayern Munich/Senegal):** A versatile winger who can play on either flank, known for his pace, direct running, and clinical finishing.
- **Raheem Sterling (Chelsea/England):** A pacy and skillful winger with excellent dribbling ability, movement off the ball, and goal-scoring instincts.
- **Vinícius Júnior (Real Madrid/Brazil):** A young and dynamic winger with incredible pace, dribbling skills, and the ability to take on defenders.

These are just a few examples of the diverse range of wing players in the modern game. Each player brings their unique style and skill set to the position, making it one of the most exciting and unpredictable roles in soccer.

Attacking Midfielders

The attacking midfielder (AM) is the creative spark plug in a team's offense, responsible for unlocking defenses and crafting scoring opportunities. Their role has evolved in modern soccer, demanding a blend of technical finesse, tactical intelligence, and a keen eye for goal. Let's look into the multifaceted responsibilities of this influential position:

Playmaking and Creativity: The AM is the team's chief playmaker, tasked with creating chances for their teammates. They possess exceptional vision, passing range, and the ability to thread through balls that dissect defenses. Their creativity manifests in their ability to find unique solutions to unlock packed defenses, often through unexpected passes, clever flicks, or perfectly weighted through balls.

Dribbling and Ball Control: AMs are often tasked with carrying the ball forward from midfield into the attacking third. Their dribbling skills allow them to navigate tight spaces, beat defenders, and attract attention, thus creating space for their teammates. Their ability to maintain possession under pressure is crucial for maintaining attacking momentum.

Shooting and Goal-Scoring Threat: While their primary role is to create, AMs are also expected to be a goal-scoring threat. They often arrive late in the box to unleash shots from distance or capitalize on rebounds. Their ability to find the back of the net adds another layer to their game, making them more unpredictable and difficult to defend against.

Finding Pockets of Space: AMs must possess excellent spatial awareness, constantly seeking pockets of space between the lines of the opposition's defense and midfield. These pockets allow them to receive the ball in dangerous areas, turn, and create chances for themselves or their teammates. Their movement off the ball is just as important as their actions on the ball.

Transitional Play: AMs are critical in transitional moments, both from defense to attack and vice versa. They must be able to quickly react to changes in possession, either by pressing the opposition high up the pitch or launching counterattacks with incisive passes. Their adaptability and decision-making in these transitional phases can be game-changing.

Set-Piece Specialist: AMs are often tasked with taking free kicks and corners due to their technical ability and precision. Their deliveries can be the difference between a goal and a missed opportunity. They must be able to vary their delivery, providing both in-swinging and out-swinging crosses, as well as direct shots on goal.

Leadership and Communication: AMs are often vocal leaders on the pitch, organizing the attack and communicating with their teammates. Their ability to inspire and motivate their fellow players is essential for maintaining a cohesive and effective attacking unit.

Different Types of Attacking Midfielders:

- **Classic Number 10 (Trequartista):** These players are the traditional playmakers, operating in the space between the midfield and attack. They possess exceptional vision, passing range, and technical skills.
- **False Nine:** These players are strikers who drop deep into midfield, dragging defenders out of position and creating space for attacking midfielders to exploit.
- **Advanced Playmaker:** These players are similar to the classic number 10 but operate in a more advanced position, closer to the strikers.
- **Shadow Striker:** These players operate behind the main striker, looking to link up play and create chances through movement and passing.

Examples of Modern Attacking Midfielders:

- **Kevin De Bruyne (Manchester City/Belgium):** A complete attacking midfielder with exceptional vision, passing range, and goal-scoring ability.
- **Bruno Fernandes (Manchester United/Portugal):** A dynamic and creative midfielder known for his goals, assists, and leadership qualities.
- **Martin Odegaard (Arsenal/Norway):** A technically gifted playmaker with exceptional dribbling skills, vision, and the ability to unlock defenses.
- **Phil Foden (Manchester City/England):** A versatile attacking midfielder who can play in various positions, known for his close control, dribbling, and passing.
- **James Maddison (Tottenham Hotspur/England):** A creative and intelligent midfielder with excellent set-piece delivery and an eye for goal.

Strikers

Strikers, the spearhead of a team's attack, are the players tasked with the ultimate responsibility: scoring goals. In modern soccer, their role has expanded beyond simply finishing chances, demanding a diverse skill set that combines technical prowess, tactical intelligence, and physical attributes. Let's explore the multifaceted responsibilities of this crucial position:

Goalscoring: First and foremost, strikers must be clinical finishers. They must possess a variety of techniques to find the back of the net, whether it's through powerful strikes, delicate chips, or precise headers. They must be able to convert half-chances into goals, as well as score spectacular goals when the opportunity arises. Their composure in front of goal is often the difference between victory and defeat.

Movement and Positioning: Strikers must constantly move to create space for themselves and their teammates. This involves making intelligent runs off the ball, finding gaps in the defense, and anticipating where the ball will be played. Their movement creates confusion for defenders, opening up passing lanes and creating opportunities for shots on goal.

Hold-Up Play and Link-Up Play: Strikers must be able to hold up the ball under pressure, allowing their teammates to join the attack. This requires strength, balance, and good control. They must also be able to link up play with their midfielders and wingers, using their passing ability to create combinations and unlock defenses.

Pressing and Defensive Contributions: In modern soccer, strikers are expected to contribute to the team's defensive efforts. They initiate the press from the front, putting pressure on the opposition's defenders and forcing them into mistakes.

Their work rate and defensive discipline are crucial for winning back possession high up the pitch and launching quick counterattacks.

Aerial Threat: Strikers must be a threat in the air, both in attacking and defensive situations. They must be able to win aerial duels in the opposition's box to score goals from crosses and set-pieces. They should also be able to defend aerial balls in their own box to prevent the opposition from creating chances.

Tactical Awareness: Strikers must have a good understanding of the game's tactical nuances. They need to know when to drop deep to link up play, when to make runs in behind the defense, and when to hold their position to occupy defenders. Their tactical intelligence allows them to adapt to different game situations and make the right decisions to help their team.

Different Types of Strikers:

- **Poacher:** These strikers have a knack for being in the right place at the right time, often scoring tap-ins and close-range goals.
- **Target Man:** These strikers are tall and strong, using their physicality to hold up the ball, win aerial duels, and create chances for their teammates.
- **Complete Forward:** These strikers possess a combination of skills, including finishing, hold-up play, dribbling, and passing.
- **False Nine:** These strikers drop deep into midfield, dragging defenders out of position and creating space for attacking midfielders to exploit.

Examples of Modern Strikers:

- **Erling Haaland (Manchester City/Norway):** A prolific goal-scorer with exceptional pace, strength, and finishing ability.
- **Kylian Mbappé (Paris Saint-Germain/France):** A lightning-fast and skillful striker with a devastating combination of speed, dribbling, and finishing.
- **Robert Lewandowski (Barcelona/Poland):** A complete striker with exceptional technique, movement, and finishing ability.
- **Harry Kane (Tottenham Hotspur/England):** A versatile striker who can score from anywhere on the pitch, known for his hold-up play, passing, and vision.
- **Karim Benzema (Real Madrid/France):** A clinical finisher with exceptional movement, link-up play, and the ability to create chances for himself and his teammates.

These strikers represent the diversity of the modern striker's role. They showcase the various skills and attributes needed to thrive in today's game.

CHAPTER 2: FORMATIONS AND THEIR EVOLUTION

Classic Formations: 4-4-2, 3-5-2

Classic formations like the 4-4-2 and 3-5-2 have stood the test of time, leaving an indelible mark on soccer tactics. Let's look into these formations, exploring their structure, strengths, weaknesses, and evolution in the modern game.

4-4-2: The Timeless Classic

The 4-4-2 formation, featuring four defenders, four midfielders, and two strikers, is a soccer staple renowned for its balance and simplicity.

* **Structure:** Two central defenders anchor the defense, flanked by two fullbacks. Two central midfielders control the middle of the park, while two wide midfielders provide width and support in both attack and defense. Two strikers lead the line, combining to create scoring opportunities.
* **Strengths:** The 4-4-2 offers a solid defensive structure, with two banks of four providing a compact shape that is difficult to break down. It also offers a balanced attacking threat, with two strikers providing a focal point in the box and the wide midfielders offering width and crosses.
* **Weaknesses:** The 4-4-2 can be vulnerable to teams with numerical superiority in midfield, as the two central midfielders may be outnumbered and overrun. Additionally, the formation can lack creativity in midfield if the wide midfielders are primarily tasked with defensive duties.
* **Evolution:** In modern soccer, the 4-4-2 has evolved to become more fluid and adaptable. Fullbacks often push high up the pitch, acting as auxiliary wingers, while one of the central midfielders may join the attack to create an overload in the final third. This evolution has allowed the 4-4-2 to remain relevant in contemporary soccer.

3-5-2: The Italian Stallion

The 3-5-2 formation, featuring three central defenders, five midfielders, and two strikers, is a tactically intriguing system that offers defensive solidity and attacking flexibility.

* **Structure:** Three central defenders form a back three, providing a solid foundation for the team. Two wing-backs operate on the flanks, offering both defensive cover and attacking width. Three central midfielders control the middle of the park, with one often acting as a deep-lying playmaker and the other two providing box-to-box dynamism. Two strikers lead the line, often playing close together to combine and create chances.

- **Strengths:** The 3-5-2 offers excellent defensive stability with three central defenders and two wing-backs. It also provides numerical superiority in midfield, allowing the team to control possession and dictate the tempo of the game. The wing-backs offer an attacking outlet, while the two strikers provide a focal point in the box.
- **Weaknesses:** The 3-5-2 can be vulnerable to counterattacks if the wing-backs are caught high up the pitch. Additionally, the formation can lack width in attack if the wing-backs are primarily tasked with defensive duties.
- **Evolution:** In modern soccer, the 3-5-2 has evolved to become more fluid and adaptable. The wing-backs often push high up the pitch, acting as wingers, while one of the central midfielders may drop between the center backs to create a temporary back four in defense. This evolution has made the 3-5-2 a popular choice for teams seeking to combine defensive solidity with attacking potency.

Overall, the 4-4-2 and 3-5-2 formations are classic examples of tactical systems that have stood the test of time. While they may have evolved and adapted to the demands of modern soccer, their fundamental principles of balance, structure, and flexibility remain relevant.

Modern Adaptations: 4-3-3, 4-2-3-1

Modern soccer tactics have evolved rapidly, giving rise to dynamic and adaptable formations like the 4-3-3 and 4-2-3-1. These systems have become popular choices for coaches seeking to balance defensive solidity with attacking creativity. Let's look into these formations, exploring their structure, strengths, weaknesses, and variations in the modern game.

4-3-3: The Fluid Formation

The 4-3-3 formation, featuring four defenders, three midfielders, and three forwards, is a versatile system that offers a blend of defensive stability and attacking flair.

- **Structure:** A back four anchors the defense, consisting of two central defenders and two fullbacks. Three central midfielders control the middle of the park, with one often acting as a defensive anchor and the other two providing a mix of creativity and defensive cover. Three forwards lead the line, typically comprising two wingers and a central striker.
- **Strengths:** The 4-3-3 offers defensive solidity with a back four and a dedicated holding midfielder. It also provides ample attacking options, with three forwards who can combine to create chances and the midfielders supporting the attack. The formation's fluidity allows for quick transitions

between defense and attack, making it ideal for teams that want to play a high-tempo, pressing style.
- **Weaknesses:** The 4-3-3 can be vulnerable if the opposition exploits the space behind the fullbacks. Additionally, the formation can lack defensive cover in midfield if the two attacking midfielders are not diligent in their defensive duties.
- **Variations:** The 4-3-3 has several variations, including:
  - **4-3-3 Holding:** This variation features a defensive midfielder who sits in front of the defense, providing extra protection and allowing the other two midfielders to push forward.
  - **4-3-3 Attacking:** This variation sees the midfielders push higher up the pitch, offering more support to the attack.
  - **4-3-3 False 9:** This variation features a striker who drops deep into midfield, creating space for the wingers to exploit.

4-2-3-1: The Balanced Formation

The 4-2-3-1 formation, featuring four defenders, two holding midfielders, three attacking midfielders, and one striker, is a balanced system that offers both defensive stability and attacking creativity.

- **Structure:** A back four provides defensive solidity, while two holding midfielders shield the defense and initiate build-up play. Three attacking midfielders operate behind a lone striker, offering a variety of attacking options. The wingers provide width and crosses, while the central attacking midfielder acts as a playmaker or a goal-scoring threat.
- **Strengths:** The 4-2-3-1 offers a good balance between defense and attack. The two holding midfielders provide a strong defensive base, while the three attacking midfielders offer creativity and goal-scoring threat. The formation is also adaptable, allowing teams to play with a high press or a deeper defensive block.
- **Weaknesses:** The 4-2-3-1 can be vulnerable to counterattacks if the holding midfielders are caught out of position. Additionally, the formation can lack width if the wingers are not effective in stretching the opposition's defense.
- **Variations:** The 4-2-3-1 has several variations, including:
  - **4-2-3-1 Wide:** This variation features wingers who stay wide, providing crosses into the box.
  - **4-2-3-1 Narrow:** This variation sees the attacking midfielders play in a more central position, creating a compact attacking unit.
  - **4-2-3-1 False 9:** This variation features a striker who drops deep into midfield, creating space for the attacking midfielders to exploit.

The 4-3-3 and 4-2-3-1 formations are examples of modern tactical systems that offer a blend of defensive solidity and attacking creativity. Their adaptability and flexibility make them popular choices for coaches at all levels of the game.

Innovative Setups: 3-4-3, 3-4-2-1

Modern soccer tactics have seen the resurgence of three-at-the-back formations like the 3-4-3 and 3-4-2-1, which offer unique advantages in both defense and attack. These formations provide a blend of defensive solidity, midfield control, and attacking flexibility, making them increasingly popular choices for coaches seeking innovative tactical setups. Let's explore their structure, strengths, weaknesses, and variations in the modern game.

3-4-3: The Dynamic Formation

The 3-4-3 formation, featuring three central defenders, four midfielders, and three forwards, is a versatile system that offers a unique balance of defensive strength and attacking firepower.

- **Structure:** Three central defenders form a solid backline, providing a defensive foundation. Two wing-backs operate on the flanks, offering both defensive cover and attacking width. Two central midfielders control the middle of the park, often in a double-pivot configuration, providing both defensive cover and the ability to launch attacks. Three forwards lead the line, typically comprising two wingers or inside forwards and a central striker.
- **Strengths:** The 3-4-3 offers defensive solidity with three central defenders, while the wing-backs provide additional defensive cover. The formation's midfield strength allows for control of possession and the ability to dictate the tempo of the game. With three forwards and attacking wing-backs, the 3-4-3 offers a potent attacking threat, creating opportunities through wide play, combination play, and direct runs.
- **Weaknesses:** The 3-4-3 can be vulnerable if the opposition exploits the space behind the wing-backs. Additionally, the formation can lack defensive cover in wide areas if the wing-backs are caught high up the pitch.
- **Variations:** The 3-4-3 has several variations, including:
    - **3-4-3 Diamond:** This variation features a diamond midfield shape, with one holding midfielder, two central midfielders, and one attacking midfielder.
    - **3-4-3 Flat:** This variation features a flat midfield line, with two holding midfielders and two more advanced midfielders.

3-4-2-1: The Tactical Chameleon

The 3-4-2-1 formation, a variation of the 3-4-3, offers a slightly different tactical approach, emphasizing midfield control and creative play.

- **Structure:** Like the 3-4-3, this formation features a back three and two wing-backs. However, it differs in midfield, where two central midfielders are deployed in a double pivot, and two attacking midfielders operate behind a lone striker.
- **Strengths:** The 3-4-2-1 offers defensive solidity similar to the 3-4-3, but with an added emphasis on midfield control. The two attacking midfielders provide creativity and goal-scoring threat, while the lone striker acts as a focal point for the attack. This formation is adaptable, allowing teams to play with a high press or a deeper defensive block, depending on the game situation.
- **Weaknesses:** Similar to the 3-4-3, the 3-4-2-1 can be vulnerable to counterattacks if the wing-backs are caught out of position. Additionally, the formation can lack defensive cover in wide areas if the wing-backs are not diligent in their tracking back.

Overall, the 3-4-3 and 3-4-2-1 formations are innovative tactical setups that offer a unique blend of defensive solidity, midfield control, and attacking threat. Their adaptability and flexibility make them popular choices for coaches seeking to gain a competitive edge.

CHAPTER 3: ATTACKING PLAY IN MODERN SOCCER

Building from the Back

Building from the back is a fundamental tactical approach in modern soccer, emphasizing patient and controlled possession from the defensive third to launch attacks. It's a philosophy rooted in retaining the ball, creating numerical superiority, and exploiting spaces to progress up the field. Let's break down the key elements and principles of building from the back:

Goalkeeper as the First Attacker: The goalkeeper is no longer just a shot-stopper; they are the first attacker in a possession-based system. Goalkeepers must be comfortable with the ball at their feet, possess excellent passing range, and make intelligent decisions under pressure. Their ability to initiate attacks from deep can catch opponents off guard and create opportunities for quick transitions.

Center Backs as Playmakers: Modern center backs are not just defenders; they are also playmakers. They must be comfortable receiving the ball under pressure, possess excellent passing skills, and have the vision to find teammates in advanced positions. Their ability to break lines with accurate long passes or dribble into midfield can unlock defenses and create numerical superiority in attacking areas.

Fullbacks as Outlets: Fullbacks have an important role in building from the back by providing width and attacking options. They push high up the pitch, offering themselves as passing outlets for the goalkeeper and center backs. They must be comfortable receiving the ball in tight spaces, possess good technical ability, and have the vision to find teammates in advanced positions.

Midfielders as Facilitators: Midfielders are the engines of a team's build-up play. They move intelligently to create passing triangles and offer support to the defenders and fullbacks. They must be comfortable receiving the ball under pressure, possess excellent ball control and passing skills, and have the vision to find forward passing options.

Numerical Superiority: Building from the back is all about creating numerical superiority in different areas of the pitch. By overloading the defensive third, teams can attract the opposition's press and create space in other areas. This numerical advantage allows for safe and controlled possession, creating opportunities to progress the ball up the field.

Exploiting Spaces: Building from the back is not just about keeping possession; it's about finding ways to exploit spaces and break down the opposition's defensive structure. This can be achieved through quick combinations, one-two passes, third-man runs, or switching the play to exploit the weak side.

Patience and Discipline: Building from the back requires patience and discipline. Teams must be willing to circulate the ball patiently, probing for weaknesses in the opposition's defense. They must also be disciplined in their positioning and movement, maintaining a compact shape and avoiding risky passes that could lead to turnovers.

Risk vs. Reward: Building from the back carries an inherent risk, as losing possession in the defensive third can lead to dangerous counterattacks. However, the potential rewards of creating scoring opportunities and controlling the game's tempo outweigh the risks for many teams.

Examples of Teams That Build from the Back:

* **Manchester City:** Under Pep Guardiola, Manchester City has perfected the art of building from the back, dominating possession and creating a multitude of scoring chances.
* **Barcelona:** Barcelona's tiki-taka style of play is synonymous with building from the back, with their intricate passing and movement creating a mesmerizing spectacle.
* **Bayern Munich:** Bayern Munich's high-pressing and possession-based style relies heavily on building from the back to control the game and create opportunities.
* **Liverpool:** Under Jurgen Klopp, Liverpool has adopted a high-intensity pressing style that often starts with building from the back to lure opponents into traps.

Patterns of Play in the Final Third

The final third is where soccer matches are won and lost. It's the attacking zone where teams unleash their creativity, exploit spaces, and ultimately, aim to score goals. Let's explore some common patterns of play in the final third, highlighting the tactical intricacies and strategies that teams employ to break down stubborn defenses.

Wide Play and Crossing:

One of the most traditional and effective patterns of play in the final third is utilizing the wings. Wingers hug the touchline, dribble past defenders, and deliver crosses into the box. This pattern relies on the width provided by the wingers, the accuracy of their crosses, and the movement of attackers in the box to meet the ball. Modern variations of this pattern include early crosses, cutbacks, and low-driven crosses that aim to create chaos in the penalty area.

Combination Play in Central Areas:

Teams often focus on intricate passing combinations in central areas to penetrate the final third. This pattern involves quick one-twos, third-man runs, and interchanges between midfielders and forwards. The aim is to create overloads in central areas, draw defenders out of position, and find gaps to exploit. This pattern demands technical skill, quick decision-making, and excellent spatial awareness from the players.

Through Balls and Runs in Behind:

A direct and effective way to penetrate the final third is through well-timed through balls that exploit the space behind the opposition's defense. Strikers and attacking midfielders make runs in behind the defensive line, aiming to latch onto these passes and create one-on-one opportunities with the goalkeeper. This pattern requires precise passing, intelligent movement, and anticipation from both the passer and the receiver.

Counter-Attacking:

Counter-attacks are a potent weapon in the final third, exploiting the space left behind by the opposition as they push forward. Teams that excel at counter-attacking rely on quick transitions, pacey players, and decisive decision-making. They often look to catch the opposition off-balance and create scoring chances with swift and direct attacks.

Set-Pieces:

Set-pieces, such as corners and free-kicks, are vital opportunities to score goals in the final third. Teams devote significant time to practicing set-piece routines, utilizing various strategies like short corners, decoy runs, and zonal marking to create chaos and exploit defensive weaknesses. The delivery of the set-piece and the movement of the attackers in the box are critical factors in converting these chances into goals.

Individual Brilliance:

Sometimes, a moment of individual brilliance can unlock a stubborn defense. A mazy dribble, a stunning long-range shot, or a clever piece of skill can create a goal out of nothing. While not a pattern of play per se, individual brilliance can be the deciding factor in tight matches.

Adaptability and Variation:

Successful teams don't rely on just one pattern of play in the final third. They are adaptable and can vary their approach depending on the opposition's strengths and weaknesses. They might switch between wide play and central penetration, or utilize counter-attacks when the opportunity arises. The key is to have a diverse range of attacking options and the flexibility to adapt to different game situations.

Use of Overloads and Underloads

Modern soccer tactics have evolved to embrace the concepts of overloads and underloads, which are strategic manipulations of numerical superiority or inferiority in specific areas of the pitch. These concepts are used to gain a tactical advantage, create space, and ultimately, unlock stubborn defenses. Let's look into how teams use overloads and underloads to create attacking opportunities.

Overloads: Creating Numerical Superiority

Overloads occur when a team intentionally positions more players in a particular zone than the opposition. This creates a numerical advantage, allowing the team in possession to control the ball, attract defenders, and exploit the space that opens up elsewhere on the pitch.

- **Wide Overloads:** Teams often overload the flanks by pushing fullbacks high up the pitch and instructing wingers to hug the touchline. This stretches the opposition's defense horizontally, creating space in central areas for midfielders or forwards to exploit.
- **Central Overloads:** Teams can create overloads in central areas by instructing central midfielders to join the attack and by having strikers drop deep to receive the ball. This can overwhelm the opposition's midfield, creating opportunities for through balls, shots, or passes to players in wide positions.
- **Combinations and Triangles:** Overloads are often created through intricate passing combinations and triangles. By quickly exchanging passes in tight spaces, teams can draw defenders out of position and create openings for penetrative passes or shots.

Benefits of Overloads:

- **Maintaining Possession:** Overloads allow teams to keep possession of the ball, controlling the tempo of the game and frustrating the opposition.
- **Creating Space:** By attracting defenders to the overloaded zone, teams create space in other areas of the pitch, which can be exploited by attackers.

- **Creating Goal-Scoring Opportunities:** Overloads can lead to goal-scoring chances through combinations, crosses, or shots from distance.

Underloads: Creating Space Through Numerical Inferiority

Underloads occur when a team intentionally positions fewer players in a particular zone than the opposition. This creates a numerical disadvantage but can also open up space for other players to exploit.

- **Underloads in Wide Areas:** A team might leave one winger isolated against two defenders, creating an underload. However, this can be a deliberate tactic to draw the defenders out wide, creating space in central areas for other attackers to exploit.
- **Underloads in Central Areas:** A team might leave one central midfielder isolated against two opponents, creating an underload. This can be done to attract the opposition's press and create space for the fullbacks to advance into midfield.

Benefits of Underloads:

- **Attracting the Press:** Underloads can lure the opposition into pressing high up the pitch, leaving space behind their defensive line.
- **Creating Space:** By occupying defenders in the underloaded zone, teams create space elsewhere on the pitch, which can be exploited by other attackers.
- **Creating Goal-Scoring Opportunities:** Underloads can lead to goal-scoring chances through quick transitions, counterattacks, or through balls to players in space.

Combining Overloads and Underloads:

Successful teams often combine overloads and underloads to create complex attacking patterns. For example, a team might create an overload on one flank to attract defenders, then quickly switch the play to the underloaded flank to exploit the space that has opened up. This requires quick decision-making, accurate passing, and intelligent movement from the players.

False Nines and Their Influence

The false nine is a tactical innovation that has revolutionized attacking play in modern soccer. It's a role that challenges the traditional notion of a striker, offering a unique blend of creativity, movement, and tactical flexibility. Let's look into the concept of the false nine and explore its impact on the modern game.

What is a False Nine?

A false nine is a center forward who, instead of leading the line as a traditional striker, drops deep into midfield to participate in the build-up play. This movement disrupts the opposition's defensive structure, creates space for other attackers, and allows for greater fluidity in the team's attacking movements.

Key Attributes of a False Nine:

- **Technical Ability:** False nines must possess exceptional ball control, passing accuracy, and dribbling skills. They often receive the ball under pressure in tight spaces, so they need to be able to quickly turn and find a teammate.
- **Vision and Creativity:** False nines must have excellent vision and creativity to unlock defenses. They need to be able to see passing lanes that others might miss and create scoring opportunities for their teammates.
- **Movement and Intelligence:** False nines must be intelligent movers, constantly seeking pockets of space between the lines of the opposition's defense and midfield. Their movement off the ball is just as important as their actions on the ball.
- **Versatility:** False nines must be versatile players who can adapt to different game situations. They need to be able to drop deep to link up play, make runs in behind the defense, and even track back to help out defensively.

Tactical Advantages of a False Nine:

- **Disrupting Defensive Structure:** The false nine's movement away from the traditional striker position forces the opposition's defenders to make difficult decisions. Do they follow the false nine deep, leaving space behind them? Or do they stay in position, allowing the false nine to receive the ball in dangerous areas?
- **Creating Space for Other Attackers:** The false nine's movement creates space for other attackers, such as wingers and attacking midfielders, to exploit. This can lead to overloads in wide areas or in the space behind the defense.
- **Increasing Fluidity and Unpredictability:** The false nine's presence makes the team's attack more fluid and unpredictable. The opposition can't simply focus on marking one player; they have to be aware of the movement of all the attackers.

Examples of Successful False Nines:

- **Lionel Messi (Barcelona/Argentina):** Lionel Messi, under Pep Guardiola at Barcelona, is the quintessential example of a false nine. His movement, dribbling, and passing caused havoc for defenses around the world, leading to numerous titles and accolades.

- **Roberto Firmino (Liverpool/Brazil):** Roberto Firmino's role as a false nine at Liverpool under Jurgen Klopp has been crucial to the team's success. His intelligent movement, pressing, and link-up play have made him an invaluable asset.
- **Francesco Totti (Roma/Italy):** Francesco Totti, during his time at Roma, was one of the pioneers of the false nine role. His creativity, vision, and finishing ability made him a nightmare for defenders.

The Future of the False Nine:

The false nine is a tactical innovation that has changed the way we think about attacking play in soccer. It's a role that continues to evolve, with new variations and interpretations emerging all the time. As the game becomes more tactical and complex, the false nine is likely to remain a key component of many teams' attacking strategies.

Inside Forwards vs. Traditional Wingers

Modern soccer tactics have led to a fascinating evolution of attacking wide players, blurring the lines between traditional wingers and inside forwards. While both roles share similarities, their distinct movements, responsibilities, and tactical impact create unique dynamics on the pitch. Let's explore the nuances of these two positions and how they contribute to a team's attacking play.

Traditional Wingers: The Speedsters and Crossers

Traditional wingers, often deployed in wide positions in formations like 4-4-2 or 4-3-3, are known for their speed, directness, and ability to deliver crosses into the box.

- **Movement:** They hug the touchline, staying wide to stretch the opposition's defense horizontally. They use their pace and dribbling skills to beat defenders on the outside and deliver crosses into the penalty area.
- **Responsibilities:** Their primary role is to create scoring opportunities through crosses, cutbacks, and low-driven balls into the box. They are also expected to track back and help out defensively, covering their fullbacks and preventing counterattacks.
- **Strengths:** Traditional wingers excel at creating width, stretching the defense, and delivering crosses. Their pace and dribbling skills can be devastating in one-on-one situations.
- **Weaknesses:** They can be predictable, as their movements are often focused on getting to the byline and crossing the ball. They may also

struggle to contribute in central areas and lack the creativity of inside forwards.

Inside Forwards: The Creative Playmakers

Inside forwards, often deployed in formations like 4-3-3 or 4-2-3-1, are more versatile attackers who operate in the half-spaces between the wing and the center of the pitch.

* **Movement:** They tend to drift inside from wide positions, looking to combine with midfielders and forwards in central areas. They use their dribbling skills, close control, and vision to create chances through through balls, incisive passes, and shots on goal.
* **Responsibilities:** Their primary role is to create scoring opportunities for themselves and their teammates through combinations, dribbles, and shots. They also contribute to the build-up play by linking up with midfielders and creating overloads in central areas.
* **Strengths:** Inside forwards are creative and unpredictable attackers who can operate effectively in both wide and central areas. Their dribbling skills, passing ability, and vision make them difficult to defend against.
* **Weaknesses:** They may not provide the same width as traditional wingers, which could make it easier for the opposition to defend the flanks. They also need to be aware of their defensive responsibilities, as their tendency to drift inside can leave space for opposition counterattacks.

The Tactical Impact of Wingers vs. Inside Forwards

The choice between a traditional winger and an inside forward depends on the team's overall tactical approach and the specific qualities of the players.

* **Width vs. Central Penetration:** Traditional wingers offer more width and crossing ability, while inside forwards provide more creativity and goal-scoring threat in central areas.
* **Directness vs. Combination Play:** Traditional wingers often rely on direct runs and crosses, while inside forwards thrive in combination play with midfielders and forwards.
* **Defensive Responsibilities:** Both roles have defensive responsibilities, but traditional wingers typically have more defensive duties due to their wider positioning.

Examples:

* **Traditional Wingers:** Leroy Sané (Bayern Munich), Kingsley Coman (Bayern Munich), and Rafael Leão (AC Milan)

- **Inside Forwards:** Mohamed Salah (Liverpool), Heung-Min Son (Tottenham Hotspur), and Bernardo Silva (Manchester City)

Overall, in modern soccer, the distinction between traditional wingers and inside forwards has become increasingly blurred. Many players possess the skills and attributes to excel in both roles, offering managers tactical flexibility and a variety of attacking options.

Role of the Target Man

The target man, a classic yet evolving role in soccer, offers a unique dimension to a team's attacking strategy. Traditionally associated with physical presence and aerial dominance, the modern target man has expanded their skillset to become a versatile and influential figure on the pitch. Let's look into the multifaceted role of the target man in modern soccer.

Physical Presence and Aerial Dominance: The target man's imposing physique and aerial prowess are their most recognizable traits. They excel at winning aerial duels, both defensively to clear the ball from their own box and offensively to flick on long balls or contest headers in the opponent's penalty area. Their ability to hold up the ball under pressure and shield it from defenders allows them to bring teammates into play and create attacking opportunities.

Link-Up Play and Lay-Offs: The target man acts as a focal point for the attack, providing a reliable outlet for long balls or passes from deep. They receive the ball with their back to goal, using their strength and body positioning to hold off defenders. From this position, they can lay off the ball to onrushing midfielders or wingers, creating space and initiating quick attacking transitions.

Creating Space and Opportunities for Others: The target man's presence alone can create opportunities for their teammates. Their ability to occupy defenders forces the opposition to adjust their defensive shape, often leaving gaps for other attackers to exploit. Additionally, their aerial threat forces defenders to stay close, limiting their ability to press higher up the pitch.

Goal Scoring Threat: While not always prolific goal-scorers, target men can still contribute significantly to their team's offensive output. They can score from headers, tap-ins, and even long-range efforts. Their physicality and ability to win aerial duels make them a constant threat in the opponent's box, especially during set-pieces.

Defensive Contributions: The target man's defensive contributions are often overlooked, but they play a vital role in the team's pressing game. Their size and strength can intimidate defenders, forcing them into mistakes. They can also use their aerial ability to win headers and clear the ball from dangerous areas.

Tactical Flexibility: Modern target men are not one-dimensional players. They are adaptable and can play in various tactical systems. Some teams use them as a lone striker in a 4-2-3-1 formation, while others pair them with a more mobile forward in a 4-4-2 or 3-5-2 system. Their tactical flexibility allows them to fit into different game plans and contribute in various ways.

Examples of Modern Target Men:

- **Harry Kane (Tottenham Hotspur/England):** Kane is a modern target man who combines physicality with exceptional technical ability and vision. He excels at hold-up play, link-up play, and finishing, making him one of the most complete strikers in the world.
- **Romelu Lukaku (Inter Milan/Belgium):** Lukaku is a powerful and athletic striker who uses his strength and speed to dominate defenders. He is a prolific goal-scorer who can also hold up the ball and bring teammates into play.
- **Olivier Giroud (AC Milan/France):** Giroud is an intelligent and experienced striker who excels at hold-up play and linking up with his teammates. He is also a threat in the air and can score crucial goals.
- **Edin Dzeko (Inter Milan/Bosnia and Herzegovina):** Dzeko is a tall and strong striker who is excellent in the air and can hold up the ball effectively. He is also a clinical finisher who can score with both his feet and head.

The target man's role in modern soccer is multifaceted and continues to evolve. They are not just big, strong players who win headers; they are intelligent, skillful, and versatile contributors who can make a significant impact on both ends of the pitch. As the game becomes more tactical and demanding, the target man's ability to adapt and evolve will be crucial for their continued success in the modern game.

CHAPTER 4: DEFENDING IN THE MODERN GAME

High Pressing Systems

High pressing is a modern defensive strategy that has transformed the way teams defend in soccer. It's an aggressive and proactive approach that involves applying intense pressure on the opposition high up the pitch, aiming to win the ball back quickly and disrupt their build-up play.

Here's how high pressing works:

- **Collective Effort:** The entire team, from strikers to defenders, participates in the press. The forwards initiate the pressure, forcing the opposition's defenders into rushed decisions or long balls. Midfielders then join the press, closing down passing lanes and preventing the opposition from advancing the ball.
- **Triggers:** Teams identify specific triggers to initiate the press. These triggers could be a misplaced pass, a poor touch, or a specific pattern in the opposition's build-up play.
- **Compactness:** Teams maintain a compact shape during the press, ensuring that there are minimal gaps between the lines of defense and midfield. This limits the space available for the opposition to operate and makes it difficult for them to find passing options.
- **Aggression and Intensity:** High pressing requires aggression and intensity. Players must be quick to close down opponents, make tackles, and win duels. They must also be willing to cover large distances and maintain a high work rate throughout the game.

Benefits of High Pressing:

- **Winning the Ball High Up the Pitch:** High pressing can lead to turnovers in the opposition's half, creating opportunities for quick counterattacks and goal-scoring chances.
- **Disrupting the Opposition's Rhythm:** By applying constant pressure, high pressing can disrupt the opposition's passing rhythm, forcing them into mistakes and preventing them from building sustained attacks.
- **Psychological Impact:** High pressing can have a demoralizing effect on the opposition, making them feel rushed and panicked.

Challenges of High Pressing:

- **Physical Demands:** High pressing is physically demanding, requiring players to cover large distances at high intensity. It's crucial for teams to have a well-conditioned squad to implement this strategy effectively.
- **Vulnerability to Counterattacks:** If the press is not executed properly, teams can be caught out of position and vulnerable to counterattacks. This is why it's important for teams to have a well-organized defensive structure behind the press.
- **Space Behind the Defense:** High pressing leaves space behind the defense, which can be exploited by teams with pacy attackers or those who can play long balls over the top.

Overall, high pressing is a complex and demanding defensive strategy, but it can be highly effective when executed properly. Teams that master this approach can dominate games, create numerous scoring opportunities, and put their opponents under immense pressure.

Compact Defending

Compact defending is a popular defensive strategy in modern soccer, prioritizing defensive organization and minimizing space for opponents to exploit. It's a proactive approach that focuses on maintaining a tight defensive shape, restricting passing lanes, and forcing the opposition into less dangerous areas.

Here's how compact defending works:

- **Narrow Defensive Shape:** Teams compress the space between their defensive and midfield lines, creating a compact block that is difficult for opponents to penetrate. This involves players staying close together, both horizontally and vertically, to limit passing options and force the opposition wide.
- **Restricting Passing Lanes:** Defenders and midfielders work in unison to close down passing lanes, intercepting passes and forcing the opposition to play backward or sideways. This disrupts their attacking rhythm and limits their ability to create goal-scoring opportunities.
- **Forcing the Opposition Wide:** Compact defending often aims to funnel the opposition's attack towards the wings, where they have less space and are further away from the goal. This makes it more difficult for them to create dangerous chances and increases the likelihood of winning the ball back.
- **Delaying and Containing:** Defenders focus on delaying the opposition's attack, buying time for their teammates to recover and regain their defensive shape. They prioritize containment over immediate tackles, forcing the opposition to make mistakes or play predictable passes.

Benefits of Compact Defending:

- **Defensive Solidity:** Compact defending creates a strong defensive structure that is difficult for opponents to break down. This minimizes the chances of conceding goals and frustrates the opposition's attacking efforts.
- **Control of the Game:** By restricting space and limiting the opposition's passing options, compact defending allows teams to control the tempo of the game and dictate the flow of play.
- **Easier to Regain Possession:** When the opposition is forced to play predictable passes in wide areas, it becomes easier for the defending team to win back possession and launch counterattacks.

Challenges of Compact Defending:

- **Vulnerability to Through Balls:** If the defensive line is not well-organized or if there are gaps between the defenders, compact defending can be vulnerable to through balls that exploit the space behind the defense.
- **Difficulty Pressing High:** Compact defending often involves a deeper defensive block, making it difficult to press the opposition high up the pitch. This can allow the opposition to build their attacks from deep and create chances through sustained possession.

Role of Defenders in Initiating Attacks

In modern soccer, defenders are no longer just stoppers; they're also starters. Their role has expanded significantly, and they are now expected to be key contributors in initiating and building attacks. Let's explore how defenders have become integral to their team's offensive strategy:

Ball-Playing Defenders:

Modern defenders are expected to be comfortable on the ball. They need to be able to receive passes under pressure, make accurate short and long passes, and even dribble out of defense when the opportunity arises. This ability to play out from the back is crucial for bypassing the opposition's press and creating numerical superiority in midfield.

Line-Breaking Passes:

Defenders with excellent vision and passing range can unlock defenses with line-breaking passes. These passes bypass the opposition's midfield and find attackers in advanced positions, creating goal-scoring opportunities. This skill is especially valuable against teams that press high up the field.

Overlapping Runs:

Full-backs are increasingly involved in attacking play, making overlapping runs down the flanks to provide width and create overloads. Their crosses into the box can be a valuable source of goals, and their ability to combine with wingers adds another dimension to the team's attacking threat.

Set-Piece Threat:

Defenders, especially center-backs, can be a significant threat from set-pieces. Their height and aerial ability make them dangerous targets for corners and free-kicks. Their ability to score goals from set-pieces can be a valuable asset for any team.

Tactical Intelligence:

Defenders need to be tactically astute to understand when to initiate attacks and when to play it safe. They must be able to read the game, identify spaces to exploit, and make quick decisions under pressure.

Examples of Defenders Who Initiate Attacks:

- **Virgil van Dijk (Liverpool):** Van Dijk is known for his composure on the ball, his ability to pick out long passes, and his forays forward into midfield.
- **Trent Alexander-Arnold (Liverpool):** Alexander-Arnold is a modern full-back who is as dangerous in attack as he is in defense. His crossing ability and playmaking skills are exceptional.
- **David Alaba (Real Madrid):** Alaba is a versatile defender who can play as a center-back or left-back. He is comfortable on the ball and often initiates attacks from deep.
- **John Stones (Manchester City):** Stones is a ball-playing center-back who is comfortable dribbling out of defense and starting attacks with his passing.

In general, the role of defenders in initiating attacks has become increasingly important in modern soccer. Defenders who possess the technical ability, tactical intelligence, and vision to contribute to the attack are highly valued assets for any team.

High Line vs. Deep Line

The positioning of a team's defensive line is a critical tactical decision that can significantly impact the game's outcome. In modern soccer, we often see two contrasting approaches: the high line and the deep line. Let's break down the key differences and considerations for each.

High Line: A Proactive Approach

A high defensive line means defenders push up the field, compressing the playing space and denying the opposition time and space on the ball. This aggressive strategy aims to:

- **Win the ball back quickly:** By pressing high, defenders can quickly regain possession and launch counterattacks.
- **Restrict space:** A high line limits the space available for the opposition to operate, making it difficult for them to build their attacks.
- **Control the game:** By maintaining a high line, teams can dictate the tempo and force the opposition into rushed decisions.

However, a high line also presents risks:

- **Vulnerability to through balls:** If the defensive line is not perfectly coordinated, a well-timed through ball can expose the space behind the defenders, leading to dangerous one-on-one situations.
- **Requires pace and organization:** A high line demands defenders with exceptional pace and a well-drilled defensive unit. Any lapse in concentration or miscommunication can be exploited by the opposition.

Deep Line: A Cautious Approach

A deep defensive line involves defenders sitting back, prioritizing defensive solidity and protecting the space behind them. This conservative strategy aims to:

- **Deny space behind the defense:** A deep line makes it difficult for the opposition to exploit the space behind the defenders, minimizing the risk of conceding goals.
- **Absorb pressure:** Teams can absorb pressure and invite the opposition to attack, looking to hit them on the counterattack.
- **Suitable for less pacey defenders:** A deep line is a viable option for teams with defenders who lack pace but possess good positional awareness and organization.

However, a deep line also has its drawbacks:

- **Inviting pressure:** A deep line can invite the opposition to attack and dominate possession, potentially leading to sustained pressure on the goal.
- **Difficulty pressing high:** With a deep line, it becomes more challenging to press the opposition high up the field, making it harder to win the ball back in advanced areas.

Choosing the Right Approach:

The decision to deploy a high line or a deep line depends on several factors, including:

- **Team's strengths and weaknesses:** A team with pacy defenders and a high-pressing style might prefer a high line, while a team with slower defenders might opt for a deep line.
- **Opposition's style of play:** If the opposition has quick attackers who thrive on through balls, a high line could be risky. Conversely, a deep line might be more suitable against a possession-oriented team.
- **Game situation:** The scoreline and time remaining in the match can also influence the choice of defensive line. A team leading by a goal might drop deeper to protect their lead, while a team trailing might push higher to create more attacking opportunities.

Ultimately, the most effective approach is one that aligns with the team's overall tactical philosophy and the specific demands of each match. By understanding the advantages and disadvantages of both high and deep lines, coaches and players can make informed decisions to maximize their team's defensive performance.

Use of Sweeper Keepers

The sweeper-keeper is a modern tactical innovation that has revolutionized the goalkeeper's role. It's a hybrid position that combines the traditional shot-stopping duties with the proactive defensive instincts of a sweeper. Let's look into how sweeper-keepers function and the impact they have on a team's defensive strategy.

Beyond the Box: Sweeper-keepers are not confined to their penalty area. They actively participate in the defensive game outside the box, acting as an extra defender. They anticipate danger, read the game, and rush off their line to intercept through balls, clear loose balls, and cut out crosses. This proactive approach helps to snuff out attacks before they become dangerous.

Distribution and Ball-Playing Skills: Sweeper-keepers are more than just shot-stoppers. They are expected to be comfortable with the ball at their feet and possess excellent passing ability. They initiate attacks from the back, distributing the ball accurately to their teammates and launching quick counterattacks. Their ball-playing skills contribute to the team's build-up play and overall possession dominance.

Communication and Organization: Sweeper-keepers are the vocal leaders of the defense. They constantly communicate with their defenders, organizing the backline, and directing their positioning. Their ability to read the game and anticipate danger allows them to provide crucial instructions to their teammates, ensuring a coordinated and disciplined defensive effort.

Risk vs. Reward: The sweeper-keeper role is not without risks. By venturing out of their penalty area, they leave the goal exposed to long-range shots or lobs. However, the reward of preventing goalscoring opportunities and initiating attacks from deep often outweighs these risks.

Tactical Fit: The sweeper-keeper role is not suitable for every team or every goalkeeper. It requires a goalkeeper with exceptional anticipation, decision-making, and technical skills. Additionally, it works best in teams that employ a high defensive line, where the sweeper-keeper's ability to cover the space behind the defense is crucial.

Examples of Sweeper Keepers:

- Manuel Neuer (Bayern Munich/Germany): Neuer is widely regarded as the pioneer of the modern sweeper-keeper role. His exceptional ability to read the game, rush out of his box, and distribute the ball has been instrumental in Bayern Munich's success.
- Ederson Moraes (Manchester City/Brazil): Ederson's calmness under pressure, distribution skills, and ability to act as a sweeper make him a perfect fit for Pep Guardiola's possession-based style of play.
- Alisson Becker (Liverpool/Brazil): Alisson combines exceptional shot-stopping ability with a sweeper-keeper mentality, making him one of the most complete goalkeepers in the world.

Defensive Compactness

Defensive compactness is a cornerstone of modern soccer tactics, emphasizing a tightly organized defensive structure to stifle opponents and limit their attacking options. It's a proactive approach that involves minimizing space between players, restricting passing lanes, and forcing the opposition into less dangerous areas of the pitch.

Here's how it works:

- **Narrow Shape:** Teams prioritize a narrow defensive shape, with players positioned close together both horizontally and vertically. This reduces the gaps between the defensive and midfield lines, making it difficult for opponents to play through the middle.
- **Closing Down Space:** Defenders and midfielders work together to quickly close down space when the opposition has the ball. This limits their time and options on the ball, forcing them to make rushed decisions or play backward passes.
- **Restricting Passing Lanes:** Players anticipate passes and position themselves to intercept or block them. This disrupts the opposition's build-up play and forces them to play long balls or riskier passes.
- **Forcing Play Wide:** Compact defending often aims to funnel the opposition's attack towards the wings, where they have less space to operate and are further away from the goal. This makes it easier for defenders to contain the attack and win back possession.
- **Collective Effort:** Compact defending requires a collective effort from the entire team. All players must be aware of their defensive responsibilities and work together to maintain the defensive shape. Communication and coordination are crucial for successful compact defending.

Benefits of Defensive Compactness:

- **Defensive Solidity:** By limiting space and restricting passing options, compact defending creates a strong defensive structure that is difficult for opponents to break down. This leads to fewer goal-scoring opportunities for the opposition.
- **Control of the Game:** Compact defending allows teams to control the tempo of the game by disrupting the opposition's rhythm and forcing them to play in areas where they are less dangerous.
- **Increased Chances of Winning the Ball Back:** By forcing the opposition into predictable passes or long balls, compact defending increases the likelihood of winning possession and launching counterattacks.

Challenges of Defensive Compactness:

- **Vulnerability to Pace and Individual Skill:** A well-organized defense can still be vulnerable to individual brilliance or the pace of a quick attacker who can exploit small spaces or beat defenders in one-on-one situations.
- **Difficult to Maintain for 90 Minutes:** Maintaining a compact defensive shape for an entire match requires a high level of fitness and concentration. Players can become fatigued, leading to lapses in concentration and gaps in the defense.

Defensive compactness is a vital aspect of modern soccer tactics. It's a proactive approach that prioritizes defensive organization and limits the opposition's attacking options. When executed effectively, it can be a game-changer, providing a solid foundation for a team's defensive strategy.

CHAPTER 5: MODERN MIDFIELD PLAY

Role of the Deep-Lying Playmaker

The deep-lying playmaker, often called a "regista" in Italian, is a midfield maestro who orchestrates a team's attacks from a deep position. Unlike traditional midfielders who focus on box-to-box running or attacking the final third, the deep-lying playmaker's primary role is to dictate the tempo and control the flow of the game from a deeper position.

Here's what makes them tick:

Position and Movement: They operate just in front of the defense, acting as the link between the backline and midfield. Their positioning is crucial for receiving the ball from defenders and initiating build-up play. They rarely venture forward, instead preferring to stay back and control the game from deep.

Passing and Vision: This is their bread and butter. Deep-lying playmakers possess exceptional passing range and accuracy, capable of spraying pinpoint long balls to switch play or threading through balls to unlock defenses. Their vision allows them to see passing lanes that others miss, creating scoring opportunities for their teammates.

Tactical Intelligence: These players have a deep understanding of the game, reading the opposition's movements and anticipating where space will open up. They make intelligent decisions under pressure, choosing the right pass to maintain possession or initiate an attack.

Defensive Awareness: While their primary role is to create, deep-lying playmakers also contribute defensively. They intercept passes, shield the backline, and position themselves to win back possession quickly if the ball is lost.

Leadership and Influence: They are often the on-field conductors, orchestrating the team's movements and dictating the tempo of the game. Their calmness and composure under pressure inspire confidence in their teammates and can demoralize opponents.

Examples of Deep-Lying Playmakers:

* **Andrea Pirlo (Italy):** A legendary regista known for his effortless passing, pinpoint accuracy, and ability to control the game's tempo.

- **Sergio Busquets (Spain):** A master of positional play and defensive awareness, Busquets is the perfect example of a modern deep-lying playmaker.
- **Toni Kroos (Germany):** Kroos is a metronomic passer with incredible vision and the ability to dictate the flow of the game from deep.
- **Jorginho (Italy):** Jorginho's composure on the ball, short passing accuracy, and ability to break lines make him a valuable deep-lying playmaker.

The deep-lying playmaker is a unique and valuable asset to any team. They are the brains of the operation, orchestrating attacks, controlling the tempo, and influencing the game from deep. Their ability to read the game, distribute the ball with precision, and maintain composure under pressure makes them one of the most important players on the pitch.

Box-to-Box Midfielders

The box-to-box midfielder is the epitome of a complete midfield player in modern soccer. Their tireless work rate, combined with a well-rounded skill set, allows them to influence every aspect of the game, from defense to attack.

Energy and Stamina: Box-to-box midfielders are the engines of the team. They cover immense distances throughout the match, constantly transitioning between defensive and attacking phases. This demands exceptional stamina and an unwavering work ethic.

Defensive Prowess: Defensively, box-to-box midfielders excel at tackling, intercepting passes, and breaking up opposition attacks. They provide crucial support to the backline, acting as a shield to protect the defensive third. Their positional awareness and reading of the game enable them to anticipate danger and snuff out attacks before they materialize.

Attacking Contribution: Box-to-box midfielders are not just defensive stalwarts; they are also potent attacking weapons. They make late runs into the box, arriving unmarked to finish off chances. Their ability to carry the ball forward, dribble past opponents, and deliver accurate passes adds a dynamic element to the team's attack.

Tactical Flexibility: These midfielders are versatile and can adapt to different tactical systems. They can play as part of a double pivot, providing defensive solidity, or as a more advanced midfielder, contributing to the attack. Their ability to seamlessly transition between defensive and attacking roles makes them invaluable assets to any team.

Examples of Box-to-Box Midfielders:

- **Jude Bellingham (Real Madrid/England):** Bellingham is a dynamic box-to-box midfielder with exceptional technical ability, athleticism, and tactical intelligence. He excels at tackling, dribbling, passing, and scoring goals.
- **Nicolò Barella (Inter Milan/Italy):** Barella is a tireless runner with a high work rate, strong tackling ability, and an eye for goal. He is equally comfortable contributing to the attack as he is breaking up opposition play.
- **Gavi (Barcelona/Spain):** Gavi is a rising star in the world of soccer, known for his exceptional ball control, passing, and dribbling skills. He is a versatile midfielder who can play in various positions, but he excels as a box-to-box midfielder.

Their combination of defensive grit, attacking prowess, and tactical flexibility makes them indispensable to any successful team. They are the engines that drive the team forward, the glue that holds the team together, and the spark that ignites the attack.

Creative Midfielders

Creative midfielders are the architects of a team's attacking play, responsible for crafting chances and unlocking stubborn defenses. Their vision, passing range, and technical ability make them the fulcrum around which the attack revolves. Let's look into the key attributes and responsibilities of these midfield maestros.

Vision and Creativity: Creative midfielders possess an innate ability to see passing lanes that others miss. They have a knack for finding pockets of space and threading through balls that split defenses wide open. Their creativity allows them to conjure up unexpected solutions, often turning a mundane possession into a goal-scoring opportunity with a single pass.

Passing Range and Accuracy: These midfielders have a wide array of passes in their arsenal. They can deliver pinpoint long balls to switch play, slide rule through balls to release attackers, or intricate short passes to break down compact defenses. Their passing accuracy is crucial for maintaining possession and building sustained attacks.

Dribbling and Close Control: Creative midfielders often possess exceptional dribbling skills. Their close control and agility allow them to navigate tight spaces, beat defenders, and attract attention, thus creating space for their teammates. Their ability to carry the ball forward can be a game-changer, as it forces the opposition to adjust their defensive shape and open up gaps.

Shooting and Goal-Scoring Threat: While their primary role is to create chances for others, creative midfielders are often capable goal-scorers themselves. They can unleash powerful shots from distance, arrive late in the box to finish off moves, or even chip the goalkeeper from delicate angles. Their goal-scoring threat adds another dimension to their game and makes them more difficult to defend against.

Set-Piece Delivery: Creative midfielders often take charge of set pieces like corners and free kicks. Their ability to deliver accurate and dangerous crosses can be a valuable source of goals. They can also take direct free kicks, posing a threat from any distance.

Examples of Creative Midfielders:

- **Kevin De Bruyne (Manchester City):** De Bruyne is the quintessential modern creative midfielder. His vision, passing range, and shooting ability make him one of the most complete players in the world.
- **Bruno Fernandes (Manchester United):** Fernandes is a dynamic and creative midfielder who excels at both creating and scoring goals. He is a master of set-piece delivery and possesses a knack for finding the back of the net.
- **Martin Odegaard (Arsenal):** Odegaard is a young and talented playmaker with exceptional vision and passing accuracy. He is known for his ability to unlock defenses with his through balls and clever passes.
- **Lorenzo Pellegrini (Roma):** Pellegrini is a versatile midfielder who can play in various roles, but he excels as a creative force behind the strikers. He possesses excellent technique, vision, and a keen eye for goal.

Creative midfielders are the heartbeat of a team's attacking play. Their vision, passing, and technical skills make them great assets to have in a squad.

CHAPTER 6: BALANCED PLAY: FINDING THE RIGHT MIX

Transitioning between Attack and Defense

Teams that excel at transitions are often the most successful, as they can dictate the tempo of the game, create scoring opportunities, and stifle the opposition's attacks. Let's break down the key elements of successful transitions:

Anticipation and Awareness: The foundation of smooth transitions lies in anticipation and awareness. Players must constantly scan the field, reading the game's flow and anticipating changes in possession. This allows them to react quickly and position themselves accordingly, whether it's to press the opponent or retreat into a defensive shape.

Counter-Pressing: One of the most effective ways to transition from attack to defense is through counter-pressing. When possession is lost, players immediately apply intense pressure on the opponent, aiming to win the ball back quickly in advanced areas. This prevents the opposition from launching a counterattack and allows the team to regain control of the game.

Compactness and Shape: Maintaining a compact shape during transitions is crucial. This means players should be close enough to each other to quickly close down space and prevent the opposition from exploiting gaps. A well-organized defensive shape makes it difficult for the opponent to find passing lanes and build their attack.

Communication: Effective communication between players is essential during transitions. Players need to communicate their intentions, whether it's to press, drop back, or switch positions. Clear communication ensures that everyone is on the same page and can react quickly to changes in the game.

Versatility: Players need to be versatile and comfortable playing in both attack and defense. This means being able to contribute to the build-up play, press the opposition, and track back to defend. Versatile players make it easier for the team to transition smoothly between phases of play.

Fitness and Mentality: Transitioning between attack and defense requires high levels of fitness and mental fortitude. Players need to be able to sprint back to defend after attacking, and they need to have the mental resilience to switch their focus quickly from one phase to the other.

Examples:

- **Liverpool:** Under Jurgen Klopp, Liverpool has become renowned for their relentless counter-pressing and quick transitions. Their ability to win the ball back high up the pitch and launch devastating counterattacks has been a key factor in their success.
- **Manchester City:** Pep Guardiola's Manchester City is known for their fluid and dynamic style of play, with seamless transitions between attack and defense. Their players are comfortable playing in both phases, making them difficult to defend against and dangerous on the counterattack.

Maintaining Shape

Maintaining shape is a fundamental tactical principle in soccer, referring to the organized positioning and spacing of players on the field to create a cohesive and effective unit. It's the tactical glue that holds a team together, ensuring defensive solidity, attacking fluidity, and seamless transitions between both phases of play.

Here's why maintaining shape is crucial:

- **Defensive Solidity:** A well-maintained shape limits the space available for opponents to exploit. Defenders stay connected, midfielders cover passing lanes, and attackers track back to support the defense. This coordinated effort makes it difficult for the opposition to penetrate and create goal-scoring opportunities.
- **Attacking Fluidity:** A well-defined shape provides a framework for attacking movements. Players understand their roles and responsibilities, knowing where to position themselves to receive passes, create triangles, and overload specific areas of the pitch. This organized movement facilitates quick ball circulation and opens up passing lanes for penetrating attacks.
- **Smooth Transitions:** Maintaining shape is essential for smooth transitions between attack and defense. When possession is lost, players quickly recognize their defensive positions and close down space, preventing the opposition from launching dangerous counterattacks. Similarly, when possession is gained, players understand their attacking roles and can quickly move into position to create goal-scoring opportunities.

Key Aspects of Maintaining Shape:

- **Compactness:** Players should maintain a compact shape, staying close enough to each other to minimize gaps and restrict space for the opposition.
- **Balance:** The team should be balanced, with players distributed evenly across the pitch. This ensures that no area is left vulnerable to exploitation.

- **Communication:** Constant communication between players is essential for maintaining shape. Players need to communicate their intentions, adjust their positions, and provide cover for each other.
- **Discipline:** Players must be disciplined in their positioning and movement, adhering to the team's tactical plan and avoiding unnecessary risks.

Examples of Teams that Excel at Maintaining Shape:

- **Atletico Madrid:** Diego Simeone's Atletico Madrid is renowned for their disciplined and compact defensive shape. They prioritize defensive solidity and are difficult to break down.
- **Manchester City:** Pep Guardiola's Manchester City is known for their fluid and dynamic positional play. They maintain a well-defined shape in both attack and defense, allowing them to control the game and create numerous scoring opportunities.

Balancing Risk and Reward

Soccer, like life, is a game of calculated risks and potential rewards. In tactical terms, balancing risk and reward is the art of making decisions that maximize the chances of success while minimizing the potential for negative consequences. It's a delicate balancing act that separates the great teams from the good ones.

Risk in Soccer Tactics:

Risk in soccer tactics can manifest in various ways. It could be a risky pass that could lead to a turnover and a counterattack, a high defensive line that could be exploited by a quick through ball, or an all-out attacking approach that leaves the team vulnerable at the back. These risks are often taken in pursuit of a greater reward, such as creating a goal-scoring opportunity or maintaining possession in dangerous areas.

Reward in Soccer Tactics:

The reward in soccer tactics is usually measured in terms of goals scored or prevented. A successful risk can lead to a goal, a change in momentum, or a tactical advantage that helps the team win the game. However, the reward is not always immediate. Sometimes, taking a calculated risk can create space for future attacks or disrupt the opposition's rhythm, leading to long-term benefits.

Factors Influencing Risk and Reward Decisions:

Several factors influence a team's decision to take risks:

- **Scoreline:** A team leading by a comfortable margin might be more conservative, while a team trailing might be more willing to take risks to chase the game.
- **Time:** As the game progresses, the risk-reward calculation changes. Teams might be more cautious in the early stages, but as time runs out, they might take more risks to secure a win or a draw.
- **Opposition:** The opposition's strengths and weaknesses play a significant role. Teams might take more risks against a weaker opponent but adopt a more cautious approach against a stronger one.
- **Team Philosophy:** Some teams, like Pep Guardiola's Manchester City, are known for their risk-taking, possession-based style, while others, like Diego Simeone's Atletico Madrid, are more pragmatic and prioritize defensive solidity.

Finding the Right Balance:

There's no one-size-fits-all approach to balancing risk and reward in soccer tactics. The optimal balance depends on the specific context of the game, the team's strengths and weaknesses, and the opposition's playing style. It's up to the coach and players to assess the situation and make informed decisions that maximize their chances of success while minimizing the potential for negative consequences.

By understanding the concept of risk and reward in soccer tactics, you'll gain a deeper appreciation for the strategic decisions made by coaches and players throughout a match.

CHAPTER 7: COUNTERATTACKS

Speed and Precision

Speed and precision are the twin engines that power a successful counterattack in modern soccer. This lightning-fast transition from defense to attack hinges on these two critical elements, exploiting the opposition's vulnerability when they are out of position and transitioning from offense to defense.

Speed: The First Strike

The essence of a counterattack is speed. Teams must act swiftly to capitalize on the moment of turnover. Players need to react instantly, bursting forward with pace and purpose. The objective is to catch the opposition off-guard, before they can reorganize their defense and close down spaces.

This rapid transition requires players with explosive acceleration and sprinting ability. Wingers and forwards, known for their speed, often are critical in counterattacks, as they can quickly exploit the space behind the opposition's high defensive line.

However, speed alone is not enough. It must be combined with intelligent movement and decision-making. Players must identify and exploit open spaces, make quick decisions about passing and dribbling, and maintain their composure under pressure.

Precision: The Finishing Touch

While speed is the catalyst for a counterattack, precision is the key to its success. Accurate passing and clinical finishing are essential for converting these rapid transitions into goals.

Players must be able to execute precise passes under pressure, finding teammates in advanced positions. The timing and weight of these passes are crucial, as they can either unlock the defense or lead to a wasted opportunity.

The final ball, whether it's a through pass, a cross, or a shot on goal, must be delivered with precision. A misplaced pass or a poorly executed shot can squander the advantage gained through speed and leave the team vulnerable to a counterattack themselves.

Examples of Speed and Precision in Counterattacks:

- **Real Madrid:** Renowned for their devastating counterattacks, Real Madrid often relies on the pace of Vinícius Júnior and Karim Benzema's clinical finishing to punish opponents.
- **Liverpool:** Under Jurgen Klopp, Liverpool has mastered the art of the counter-press, quickly winning the ball back and launching lightning-fast attacks with Mohamed Salah and Sadio Mané as their main weapons.
- **Bayern Munich:** Bayern Munich's counterattacks are a blend of speed and precision, with players like Leroy Sané and Kingsley Coman using their pace to create havoc and Thomas Müller providing the finishing touch.

Triggers for Counterattacks

Counterattacks are lightning-fast transitions from defense to offense, seizing the opportunity to catch the opposition off-balance and exploit their vulnerabilities. But what exactly triggers these swift and decisive attacks? Let's break down the key moments and situations that initiate counterattacks in modern soccer.

Turnovers and Interceptions:

The most common trigger for a counterattack is a turnover or interception. When a defending team wins the ball back, especially in their own half, it creates an immediate opportunity to launch a counterattack. The opposition is often out of position, with their players caught high up the pitch. This creates space behind their defensive line, ripe for exploitation by quick forwards and wingers.

Failed Attacks and Set-Pieces:

Failed attacks and set-pieces are another prime trigger for counterattacks. When the attacking team loses possession in the final third, their players are often out of position and vulnerable to a quick counter. Similarly, after a corner or free-kick, the attacking team's defense is often disorganized, providing an opportunity for a counterattack.

Goalkeeper Distribution:

Goalkeepers play a vital role in initiating counterattacks. A quick and accurate throw or kick from the goalkeeper can bypass the opposition's midfield and find a teammate in an advanced position. This can catch the opposition off guard and create a numerical advantage for the attacking team.

Opponent's Mistakes:

Sometimes, a simple mistake by the opposition can trigger a counterattack. A misplaced pass, a poor touch, or a miscommunication between defenders can all be exploited by an alert and opportunistic team.

Tactical Decisions:

In some cases, counterattacks are not triggered by spontaneous moments but are rather a deliberate tactical decision. Teams may intentionally sit back and absorb pressure, waiting for the right moment to launch a quick counterattack. This approach requires discipline, patience, and the ability to exploit the opposition's weaknesses.

Examples of Triggers in Action:

- **Liverpool's gegenpressing:** Jurgen Klopp's Liverpool is famous for its high-intensity pressing, which often leads to turnovers in the opposition's half. These turnovers trigger lightning-fast counterattacks led by their pacy forwards.
- **Real Madrid's transitions:** Real Madrid is known for their ability to quickly transition from defense to attack. They often win the ball back through interceptions in midfield and then unleash their speedy forwards to punish the opposition.

Role of Transition Players

Transition players are the unsung heroes of a successful counterattack. They are the bridge between defense and attack, responsible for quickly turning defensive actions into offensive opportunities. Their ability to read the game, make quick decisions, and execute precise passes can be the difference between a wasted opportunity and a goal-scoring chance.

Identifying the Transition:

The first step in a successful counterattack is recognizing the transition moment. This could be a turnover, an interception, or a loose ball. Transition players are the first to react, scanning the field for open spaces and available teammates. They must have exceptional spatial awareness and the ability to anticipate where the ball is likely to go.

Quick Decision Making:

In the fast-paced world of counterattacks, there is no time for hesitation. Transition players must make split-second decisions about where to pass the ball, who to pass it to, and when to dribble. Their ability to assess the situation and choose the best option is crucial for launching a successful counterattack.

Accurate Passing:

Precision is paramount in a counterattack. Transition players must be able to execute accurate passes under pressure, finding teammates in advanced positions. The weight and direction of these passes are critical, as they can either unlock the defense or lead to a wasted opportunity.

Vision and Creativity:

While speed and accuracy are essential, transition players also need to be creative. They must be able to see passing lanes that others miss and find innovative ways to break through the opposition's defense. This creativity can be the difference between a predictable counterattack and a devastating one.

Examples of Transition Players:

- **Kevin De Bruyne (Manchester City):** De Bruyne is a master of transitions. His ability to quickly turn defense into attack with pinpoint passes and intelligent runs has made him one of the most dangerous players in the world.
- **Luka Modric (Real Madrid):** Modric's vision, passing range, and composure under pressure make him an ideal transition player. He can quickly switch the point of attack or find a teammate with a perfectly weighted pass.
- **Joshua Kimmich (Bayern Munich):** Kimmich's versatility allows him to play as both a defensive midfielder and a right-back, making him a valuable asset in transitions. He can win the ball back defensively and then quickly launch attacks with his passing and dribbling.

CHAPTER 8: HIGH PRESS: PUTTING OPPONENTS UNDER PRESSURE

Triggers for the Press

High pressing in soccer is an aggressive defensive tactic aimed at winning the ball back quickly in the opponent's half. However, it's not just about blindly chasing the ball; it requires a coordinated effort triggered by specific cues or situations. These triggers help the team decide when and where to apply pressure, maximizing their chances of regaining possession while minimizing the risk of being caught out of position.

Let's explore some common triggers for the high press:

1. **Back Pass:** A pass from a defender back towards their own goalkeeper is a prime trigger for initiating a high press. This pass often signifies a lack of forward options for the opponent and presents an opportunity to quickly close down the goalkeeper and force a mistake or a long ball.
2. **Poor Touch or Control:** When an opponent mishandles the ball or takes a heavy touch, it's a clear sign to press. The player in possession is vulnerable, and applying immediate pressure can lead to a turnover.
3. **Lateral or Backward Pass:** Lateral or backward passes across the defensive line can also trigger a high press. These passes indicate the opponent is struggling to find a way forward and are often a sign of vulnerability.
4. **Throw-ins and Goal Kicks:** Throw-ins and goal kicks are excellent opportunities to initiate a high press. The opponent is usually less organized during these restarts, and a well-coordinated press can force them into rushed decisions or turnovers.
5. **Specific Player Movements:** Some teams identify specific player movements or patterns in the opposition's build-up play as triggers for the press. For example, a team might press when the opponent's full-backs receive the ball in wide areas or when their defensive midfielder drops deep to receive a pass from the goalkeeper.
6. **Tactical Instructions:** The coach might give specific instructions to the players regarding when to initiate the press. These instructions could be based on the scoreline, the time remaining in the match, or the opposition's playing style.

The key to successful high pressing is recognizing these triggers and reacting quickly and decisively. The entire team must be on the same page, understanding their individual roles and responsibilities within the press. By mastering the art of triggering the press, teams can create a significant advantage in terms of possession and territorial dominance, ultimately increasing their chances of winning the game.

Coordinated Pressing Movements

High pressing in soccer isn't just about running at the opponent; it's a carefully choreographed dance of coordinated movements designed to suffocate the opposition's build-up play and win the ball back as quickly as possible. Let's break down the key elements of coordinated pressing movements.

1. **The First Line of Pressure:** The forwards initiate the press, sprinting towards the ball carrier and cutting off passing lanes. They aim to force the defender into a quick decision, ideally a backward pass or a long ball that can be easily intercepted.
2. **The Second Line of Pressure:** As the forwards press, the midfielders move up in unison, forming a second line of pressure. They cover the spaces behind the forwards, preventing the opponent from finding an easy escape route. Their goal is to further limit the opponent's passing options and force them into making a mistake.
3. **The Third Line of Pressure:** The defenders also push up, maintaining a compact defensive line. They anticipate passes and position themselves to intercept or block any attempts to break the press. Their role is to provide cover for the midfielders and forwards, ensuring that the team is not exposed to counterattacks.
4. **Communication:** Constant communication between players is crucial for coordinated pressing. Players shout instructions, call for the ball, and alert their teammates to potential dangers. This communication ensures that everyone is on the same page and can react quickly to changes in the game.
5. **Flexibility and Adaptation:** Coordinated pressing is not a rigid system. Players must be flexible and adaptable, adjusting their movements and positioning based on the opponent's actions. They need to be able to quickly recognize patterns in the opposition's build-up play and adjust their press accordingly.

Examples of Coordinated Pressing Movements:

* **Liverpool's Gegenpressing:** Liverpool, under Jurgen Klopp, is renowned for their aggressive gegenpressing system. Their players swarm the opponent immediately after losing possession, suffocating them with coordinated pressure and winning the ball back quickly.
* **Manchester City's High Press:** Pep Guardiola's Manchester City employs a high-pressing system that involves coordinated movements from all players. They maintain a compact shape, close down space quickly, and force turnovers in dangerous areas.

- **Leeds United's Man-to-Man Press:** Marcelo Bielsa's Leeds United often uses a man-to-man pressing system, where each player marks a specific opponent. This requires exceptional fitness and discipline but can be highly effective in disrupting the opposition's build-up play.

Coordinated pressing movements is a complex and demanding strategy, but it can be incredibly effective in winning the ball back high up the pitch and creating goal-scoring opportunities.

Risks and Rewards

High pressing in soccer is a double-edged sword, offering both lucrative rewards and inherent risks. Teams that master this aggressive defensive tactic can reap substantial benefits, but they must also be prepared to face the potential consequences of its high-risk, high-reward nature.

Rewards of High Pressing:

- **Turnovers in Dangerous Areas:** The most immediate and obvious reward of high pressing is the ability to win the ball back high up the pitch. When the press is successful, it often leads to turnovers in the opposition's half, creating immediate goal-scoring opportunities.
- **Disrupting the Opposition's Build-up:** High pressing forces the opposition into rushed decisions and long balls, disrupting their rhythm and preventing them from building sustained attacks. This constant pressure can demoralize opponents and swing the momentum in favor of the pressing team.
- **Controlling the Game:** By winning the ball back quickly and consistently, high-pressing teams can control the tempo and territorial dominance of the match. This not only limits the opposition's chances but also puts the pressing team in a position to dictate the flow of play.

Risks of High Pressing:

- **Vulnerability to Counterattacks:** The most significant risk of high pressing is the vulnerability to counterattacks. If the press is broken, the opposition can quickly exploit the space left behind the defensive line, creating dangerous one-on-one situations or numerical superiority in attack.
- **Physical Demands:** High pressing is physically demanding, requiring players to cover large distances at high intensity throughout the match. This can lead to fatigue and lapses in concentration, potentially compromising the defensive shape and leaving the team vulnerable.
- **Requires Technical and Tactical Proficiency:** Successful high pressing requires players with excellent technical skills, tactical awareness, and the

ability to make quick decisions under pressure. A poorly executed press can easily backfire and lead to goalscoring opportunities for the opposition.

Mitigating Risks:

To mitigate the risks associated with high pressing, teams must have a well-organized defensive structure behind the press. This involves having defenders who are quick, agile, and capable of dealing with long balls and one-on-one situations. Additionally, midfielders must be disciplined in their positioning and ready to provide cover for the defenders. Effective communication and coordination between players are also crucial for minimizing the risk of counterattacks.

Balancing the aggressive nature of high pressing with a solid defensive foundation is key to maximizing its effectiveness and minimizing its potential drawbacks.

CHAPTER 9: WING PLAY IN THE MODERN GAME

Importance of Width

Width is a fundamental concept in soccer tactics, referring to the effective use of the wide areas of the pitch to create space, stretch defenses, and open up attacking opportunities. In modern soccer, where teams often prioritize central control, the importance of width cannot be underestimated.

Stretching the Defense:

One of the primary benefits of utilizing width is its ability to stretch the opposition's defense horizontally. When wingers or wide players hug the touchline and maintain a high position, they force the opposing defenders to spread out, creating gaps in central areas. This allows central attackers and midfielders to exploit the space and create goal-scoring chances.

Creating Overloads:

By utilizing the width effectively, teams can create overloads in wide areas. This involves committing more players to the flanks than the opposition, allowing them to win duels, create crossing opportunities, or cut inside to combine with central players. This numerical advantage can overwhelm defenders and lead to dangerous attacks.

Opening Up Passing Lanes:

Width not only creates space but also opens up passing lanes. When players are positioned wide, they create diagonal passing options for their teammates, making it difficult for the opposition to close down all passing channels. This facilitates ball circulation, maintains possession, and allows for more creative attacking movements.

Creating Crossing Opportunities:

Width is essential for creating crossing opportunities. Wingers who hug the touchline can receive the ball in advanced positions and deliver crosses into the box. These crosses can be aimed at strikers, who can attack the ball aerially, or at onrushing midfielders who can arrive late in the box to finish off chances.

Exploiting Defensive Weaknesses:

Wide play can be used to exploit defensive weaknesses. If the opposition's fullbacks are prone to getting caught out of position or are not strong defensively, attacking them with pace and skill can lead to significant advantages. Additionally, if the opposition is defending narrowly, utilizing the width can expose their defensive vulnerabilities and create scoring opportunities.

Examples:

* **Liverpool:** Under Jurgen Klopp, Liverpool's fullbacks, Trent Alexander-Arnold and Andrew Robertson, are known for their attacking prowess and ability to provide width, contributing significantly to the team's attacking output.
* **Bayern Munich:** Bayern Munich's wingers, Leroy Sané and Kingsley Coman, are masters at stretching the defense and creating overloads in wide areas, often leading to goals or dangerous crosses.

Width is a crucial element of modern soccer tactics. It allows teams to stretch defenses, create overloads, open up passing lanes, and create scoring opportunities. By understanding the importance of width and incorporating it into their game plan, teams can unlock the full potential of their attacking play.

Overlapping Fullbacks

Overlapping fullbacks have become a staple of modern soccer tactics, adding a dynamic attacking dimension to a position traditionally known for its defensive duties. This tactical evolution has seen fullbacks transform from defensive stalwarts into key playmakers and attacking threats.

The Overlap: A Game-Changer

The overlap occurs when a fullback makes a surging run past the winger on their side, creating an overload in wide areas and opening up new attacking options. This movement catches defenders off guard, forcing them to make difficult decisions about who to mark. The overlapping fullback can then receive the ball in advanced positions, deliver crosses into the box, or cut inside to create chances for themselves or their teammates.

Tactical Benefits:

* **Creating Width and Stretching the Defense:** Overlapping runs stretch the opposition's defense horizontally, creating space in central areas for other attackers to exploit.

- **Numerical Superiority:** By joining the attack, the fullback creates a numerical advantage in wide areas, overwhelming the opposition's defense.
- **Unpredictability:** Overlapping runs add an element of surprise to the attack, making it difficult for defenders to anticipate and react.
- **Creating Crossing Opportunities:** Overlapping fullbacks can deliver dangerous crosses into the box, providing their team with a potent attacking weapon.

When to Overlap:

The timing of an overlapping run is crucial. Fullbacks must carefully assess the situation before deciding to join the attack. They need to consider the positioning of their teammates, the opposition's defensive shape, and the space available on the flanks. A well-timed overlap can be devastating, but a poorly timed one can leave the team vulnerable to counterattacks.

Defensive Responsibilities:

While overlapping fullbacks are expected to contribute to the attack, they must also be aware of their defensive responsibilities. They need to track back quickly after an attacking move, recover their defensive position, and be prepared to defend against counterattacks.

Examples of Overlapping Fullbacks:

- **Trent Alexander-Arnold (Liverpool):** Alexander-Arnold is renowned for his attacking prowess as a right-back, regularly making overlapping runs and delivering pinpoint crosses into the box.
- **Andrew Robertson (Liverpool):** Robertson is another example of a modern fullback who excels at overlapping runs and contributing to the attack.
- **Alphonso Davies (Bayern Munich):** Davies's blistering pace and attacking instincts make him a constant threat on the left flank. His overlapping runs often create havoc for opposing defenses.

Inverted Wingers

Inverted wingers, a relatively recent tactical innovation, are wide players who operate on the opposite side of their dominant foot. This positioning creates a unique attacking dynamic, offering teams a blend of creativity, goal-scoring threat, and tactical flexibility. Let's look into the role of inverted wingers and how they're changing the landscape of wing play in modern soccer.

The Inverted Movement: Unlike traditional wingers who hug the touchline, inverted wingers drift inside from wide positions. This movement allows them to use their stronger foot to cut inside, creating shooting opportunities for themselves or playing incisive passes to teammates in the box. This unexpected movement often catches defenders off guard, opening up space and creating scoring chances.

Tactical Advantages:

- **Goal-Scoring Threat:** Inverted wingers possess a natural goal-scoring instinct. By cutting inside onto their stronger foot, they can take direct shots on goal or curl the ball into the far corner, making them a constant threat to the opposition.
- **Creative Playmaking:** Their positioning in the half-spaces allows them to combine with midfielders and forwards, creating intricate passing triangles and overloads in central areas. This can lead to through balls, cutbacks, and other creative opportunities in the final third.
- **Disrupting Defensive Shape:** Inverted wingers' movement can disrupt the opposition's defensive structure. Defenders often struggle to track their runs as they drift inside, leaving gaps that can be exploited by other attackers.

Examples of Inverted Wingers:

- **Mohamed Salah (Liverpool):** Salah is a prime example of an inverted winger who thrives on cutting inside from the right flank and unleashing powerful shots with his left foot.
- **Arjen Robben (Retired):** Robben was known for his signature move of cutting inside from the right wing and curling shots into the far corner with his left foot.
- **Son Heung-min (Tottenham Hotspur):** Son's versatility allows him to play as both a traditional winger and an inverted winger, giving his team tactical flexibility.

Considerations for Implementing Inverted Wingers:

- **Balance:** While inverted wingers offer attacking benefits, their inward movement can leave the team vulnerable on the flanks. It's crucial to have overlapping fullbacks or midfielders who can provide width and cover the space vacated by the winger.
- **Player Profile:** Not every winger is suited to the inverted role. It requires players with strong dribbling skills, the ability to shoot with both feet, and a good understanding of how to operate in central areas.

Inverted wingers are a dynamic and effective tactical option in modern soccer. Their unique movement and skill set can unlock defenses, create goal-scoring opportunities, and add a layer of unpredictability to a team's attacking play. By understanding their role and how to maximize their strengths, coaches can create potent attacking systems that can trouble even the most organized defenses.

Why Wing Play Is Less Relevant in Modern Soccer

The traditional role of the winger, once a cornerstone of attacking play, has seen a decline in prominence. While wingers still have their place in the modern game, several factors have contributed to their reduced relevance.

1. **Tactical Shifts:** Modern soccer has witnessed a shift towards possession-based systems that prioritize central control and intricate passing combinations. This often means that teams pack the midfield, leaving less space for traditional wingers to operate on the flanks. Instead, teams rely on inverted wingers or attacking fullbacks to provide width and create attacking opportunities from wider positions.
2. **Defensive Structures:** As tactical awareness and defensive organization have improved, teams have become more adept at defending against traditional wingers. Compact defensive lines, aggressive pressing, and well-drilled backlines make it difficult for wingers to isolate defenders and deliver crosses into the box. This has led to a decrease in the effectiveness of classic wing play.
3. **Rise of the False Nine:** The emergence of the false nine has further reduced the need for traditional wingers. This strikerless formation often features a central attacking midfielder who drops deep to link play, creating overloads in midfield and minimizing the reliance on wide players to create chances.
4. **Emphasis on Versatility:** Modern coaches often prefer versatile players who can operate in multiple positions. This has led to a decline in the number of out-and-out wingers, as teams increasingly opt for players who can play in central roles as well as on the flanks. This shift towards versatility has also impacted the way teams utilize their wide players, with many wingers now tasked with drifting inside to combine with midfielders and forwards.
5. **Rise of Inverted Fullbacks:** The growing popularity of inverted fullbacks has also impacted the role of wingers. These fullbacks, who tuck into midfield to create numerical superiority, often take on playmaking responsibilities that were traditionally reserved for wingers. This has led to a blurring of roles, with some wingers now operating more like inside forwards or attacking midfielders.

Despite these factors, it's important to note that wing play is not completely irrelevant in modern soccer. There are still teams that utilize traditional wingers effectively, especially those that rely on a counter-attacking style of play. However, the role of the winger has undoubtedly evolved, and their importance has diminished in many tactical systems.

As the game continues to evolve, it will be interesting to see how the role of the winger adapts further. Will we see a resurgence of traditional wing play, or will the trend towards central control and versatility continue to dominate?

CHAPTER 10: ROLE OF FULLBACKS IN THE MODERN GAME

Evolution from Defenders to Attackers

The fullback position has undergone a dramatic transformation in modern soccer, evolving from primarily defensive-minded players to dynamic contributors in both attack and defense. This tactical shift has revolutionized the way we perceive and utilize fullbacks on the pitch.

In the past, fullbacks were primarily tasked with defensive duties, focusing on marking wingers, preventing crosses, and providing cover for central defenders. Their attacking contributions were often limited to occasional overlaps and simple passes to midfielders. However, the modern game demands much more from fullbacks.

The Evolution:

The rise of possession-based football has been a major catalyst in the evolution of the fullback role. Teams now prioritize building from the back, and fullbacks are expected to be comfortable on the ball, capable of passing accurately and initiating attacks. This has led to a greater emphasis on their technical skills and decision-making under pressure.

Furthermore, the increasing importance of width in modern soccer has pushed fullbacks higher up the pitch. They are now expected to provide attacking width, overlap wingers, and deliver crosses into the box. This requires them to have excellent stamina, pace, and crossing ability.

The Modern Fullback:

The modern fullback is a hybrid player, combining defensive solidity with attacking flair. They are expected to:

* Defend effectively against wingers and attackers.
* Provide width and attacking support.
* Deliver accurate crosses into the box.
* Contribute to the build-up play from the back.
* Possess excellent stamina and physicality to cover large distances.
* Make intelligent decisions under pressure.

Examples of Modern Fullbacks:

- **Trent Alexander-Arnold (Liverpool):** Alexander-Arnold is the epitome of the modern fullback. He is a creative force from right-back, renowned for his exceptional crossing ability, vision, and passing range.
- **Andrew Robertson (Liverpool):** Robertson is another example of a modern fullback who excels in both attack and defense. He is known for his tireless running, overlapping runs, and pinpoint deliveries into the box.
- **João Cancelo (Manchester City):** Cancelo is a versatile fullback who can play on either flank. He is a technically gifted player with excellent dribbling skills and the ability to create chances for his teammates.

The evolution of the fullback from a primarily defensive role to a more attacking one is a testament to the dynamic nature of modern soccer tactics. This tactical shift has created new possibilities for teams to exploit, and it has made the fullback position one of the most exciting and influential on the pitch.

Defensive Duties

The fullback position has evolved in modern soccer, but their defensive duties remain crucial for a team's success. Let's look into the primary responsibilities fullbacks shoulder when their team is not in possession.

1. **Containing Wingers:** One of the fullback's primary responsibilities is to mark and contain the opposition's wingers. This involves tracking their runs, denying them space to receive the ball, and preventing them from delivering crosses into the box. Fullbacks must possess the pace, agility, and positional awareness to match the wingers' movements and thwart their attacking threat.
2. **One-on-One Defending:** Fullbacks often find themselves in one-on-one duels with wingers or attacking midfielders. They must be able to hold their ground, time their tackles well, and use their body positioning to force the attacker away from goal. Strong defensive technique and physicality are essential in these situations.
3. **Tracking Overlapping Runs:** As modern fullbacks venture forward to join the attack, they must also be aware of overlapping runs from their own wingers. This requires constant communication and coordination with the winger to ensure the defensive line remains compact and organized, preventing gaps for the opposition to exploit.
4. **Aerial Defending:** Fullbacks must be competent in aerial duels, both in defending crosses and winning headers in their own box during set-pieces. They need to be able to jump high, time their challenges well, and use their body strength to outmuscle opponents in the air.
5. **Defensive Positioning:** Proper defensive positioning is crucial for fullbacks. They must maintain a good distance between themselves and the center-backs to prevent gaps from opening up in the defensive line. They also need to be aware of their position relative to the rest of the team,

ensuring they are not caught out of position and leaving their team vulnerable to counterattacks.

6. **Communication and Organization:** Fullbacks play a vital role in organizing the defense. They communicate with the center-backs, midfielders, and wingers, ensuring everyone is on the same page and aware of their defensive responsibilities. They must be vocal leaders, directing their teammates and ensuring the team maintains a cohesive defensive shape.

Modern fullbacks are expected to be complete players who can contribute to both attack and defense. However, their defensive duties remain critical for a team's success. By understanding the key defensive responsibilities of fullbacks, you can gain a deeper appreciation for their importance on the pitch and their impact on the overall tactical approach of a team.

Contribution to Attack

Their involvement in the attacking phase of the game has become increasingly critical in recent years, and their contributions can be game-changing.

Overlapping Runs:

One of the most common ways fullbacks contribute to the attack is through overlapping runs. They make surging runs down the flanks, often past their own wingers, to provide width and create numerical superiority in the final third. This movement can overload the opposition's defense, opening up spaces for crosses, cutbacks, or shots on goal.

Delivering Crosses:

Fullbacks are expected to deliver accurate crosses into the box. This requires excellent technique, timing, and the ability to judge the movement of their teammates. A well-placed cross can create a goal-scoring opportunity out of nothing, making fullbacks valuable assets in the attacking third.

Creating Chances Through Dribbles and Passes:

Fullbacks with good dribbling skills can take on defenders, drawing them out of position and creating space for their teammates. They can also play incisive passes to unlock defenses and create scoring chances. Their ability to contribute to the build-up play and link up with midfielders and attackers is essential for a fluid and dynamic attacking style.

Goal-Scoring Threat:

While not their primary role, fullbacks can also chip in with goals. They often find themselves in advanced positions due to their overlapping runs, and they can capitalize on these opportunities by scoring from crosses, cutbacks, or even long-range shots. Their goal-scoring threat adds another dimension to the team's attack and makes them more difficult to defend against.

Set-Piece Delivery:

Fullbacks with good crossing ability are often tasked with taking corners and free-kicks. Their deliveries into the box can be a valuable source of goals, and they can also create havoc with their in-swinging or out-swinging crosses.

Examples of Attacking Fullbacks:

- **Trent Alexander-Arnold (Liverpool):** Alexander-Arnold is renowned for his attacking prowess as a right-back. His pinpoint crosses, vision, and passing range make him a key creative outlet for Liverpool.
- **Andrew Robertson (Liverpool):** Robertson is another attacking fullback who excels at overlapping runs and delivering dangerous crosses into the box.
- **Achraf Hakimi (PSG):** Hakimi is a dynamic fullback with blistering pace and an eye for goal. He often makes marauding runs forward and contributes significantly to his team's attacking output.
- **Theo Hernandez (AC Milan):** Hernandez is a powerful and athletic left-back who loves to get forward and join the attack. He is known for his overlapping runs, crosses, and goal-scoring ability.

In short, the modern fullback is no longer just a defender. They are an integral part of the attacking game, providing width, creativity, and goal-scoring threat. Their ability to contribute in both phases of the game makes them indispensable assets for any team.

CHAPTER 11: POSSESSION PLAY

Maintaining Possession

Maintaining possession is the cornerstone of possession-based soccer tactics, emphasizing controlled and purposeful ball circulation to dominate the game. It's more than just keeping the ball; it's about dictating the tempo, tiring out the opposition, and creating scoring opportunities through patient build-up play.

It's generally favored by the top teams, as they believe dictating possession and pace favors them more. Over a 90-minute game, this can give them more opportunities to show their superiority and increase their odds of winning.

It's analogous to flipping a coin weighted 60/40. If you only do it a few times, the odds of the 40 side winning or having equal amounts of each are quite high. However, the more you flip the coin, it becomes increasingly likely for the 60 side to win out.

Here's how teams achieve it:

1. **Short, Sharp Passing:** The foundation of possession play is quick, accurate, and short passes. This allows the team to keep the ball moving, making it difficult for the opposition to intercept or win it back. Players need to be comfortable receiving the ball under pressure and quickly distribute it to a teammate in space.
2. **Movement and Rotation:** Players constantly move and rotate positions, creating passing options and triangles for the ball carrier. This movement helps to pull defenders out of position, opening up gaps in the opposition's defense. By interchanging positions, players keep the opposition guessing and create dynamic attacking movements.
3. **Patient Build-Up:** Patience is a virtue in possession play. Teams don't rush their attacks; they patiently build up from the back, probing for weaknesses in the opposition's defense. This involves circulating the ball across the pitch, waiting for the right moment to penetrate or switch the play.
4. **Triangle Formations:** Creating triangles is essential for maintaining possession. A triangle is formed when three players are positioned in a way that allows them to easily pass the ball between each other. This creates a safe and secure passing network, making it difficult for the opposition to intercept the ball.
5. **Technical Proficiency:** Maintaining possession requires players with excellent technical skills. They need to be able to receive the ball under pressure, control it with their first touch, and pass it accurately to a teammate. A team's ability to maintain possession is directly linked to the technical ability of its players.

6. **Pressing Resistance:** Possession-based teams must be able to resist the opposition's pressing. This means being comfortable receiving the ball under pressure and having the composure to make the right decisions. It also involves having players who can dribble out of tight spaces and relieve pressure on the ball.

Examples of Teams That Excel at Maintaining Possession:

- **Manchester City:** Under Pep Guardiola, Manchester City has perfected possession-based soccer. Their intricate passing, movement, and pressing resistance have led to unprecedented success in recent years.
- **Barcelona:** Barcelona's tiki-taka style of play is synonymous with possession. Their quick, short passing and constant movement make them incredibly difficult to dispossess.
- **Spain:** The Spanish national team's success in the late 2000s and early 2010s was built on their mastery of possession football. Their tiki-taka style saw them dominate opponents and win multiple major tournaments.

Building Through the Thirds

Building through the thirds is a tactical approach in soccer that emphasizes a patient and progressive style of play, where teams aim to systematically move the ball from their own defensive third, through the midfield, and into the attacking third. This approach prioritizes possession, control, and creating scoring opportunities through well-structured attacks.

Here's how it works:

1. **First Third (Defensive Third):** The build-up begins in the defensive third, often with the goalkeeper or center-backs. The aim is to bypass the opposition's initial press and find a way to move the ball into midfield. This can be achieved through short passes, combination play, or even dribbling past the first line of pressure.
2. **Second Third (Midfield):** Once the ball reaches midfield, the team focuses on maintaining possession and progressing further up the pitch. Midfielders are critical in this phase, circulating the ball, creating passing triangles, and looking for opportunities to break lines with forward passes.
3. **Third Third (Attacking Third):** In the final third, the team aims to create goal-scoring opportunities. This involves a combination of strategies like quick passing combinations, runs in behind the defense, crosses into the box, or individual skills to create space for a shot.

Key Principles of Building Through the Thirds:

- **Patient Possession:** Teams prioritize keeping possession of the ball, even if it means playing backward or sideways passes to maintain control. This patient approach allows them to wait for the right moment to penetrate the opposition's defense.
- **Movement and Rotation:** Players constantly move and rotate positions, creating passing options and dragging defenders out of position. This dynamic movement helps to find gaps in the opposition's defense and create opportunities for forward passes.
- **Numerical Superiority:** Teams often try to create numerical overloads in different areas of the pitch, especially in midfield. This gives them an advantage in terms of passing options and makes it difficult for the opposition to win the ball back.
- **Playing Through the Lines:** Rather than relying on long balls, teams try to play through the lines of the opposition's defense. This involves finding passing lanes between defenders and midfielders, allowing them to progress the ball up the pitch in a controlled manner.

Benefits of Building Through the Thirds:

- **Control of the Game:** By maintaining possession and dictating the tempo, teams can control the game and frustrate the opposition.
- **Creating Goal-Scoring Opportunities:** Building through the thirds creates numerous chances to score, as the team can patiently probe for weaknesses in the opposition's defense and create overloads in attacking areas.
- **Limiting the Opposition's Attacking Threat:** By keeping possession, the team denies the opposition the opportunity to attack, reducing their chances of scoring.

Building through the thirds is a sophisticated and effective tactical approach that emphasizes possession, control, and patient build-up play. It's a style of play that requires technical skill, tactical intelligence, and teamwork, but it can be incredibly rewarding when executed properly.

Importance of Ball Retention

Ball retention is the lifeblood of possession-based soccer. It's more than just keeping the ball; it's a strategic tool that empowers teams to control the game, create scoring chances, and frustrate opponents. Let's explore why ball retention is so vital in modern tactics.

Control and Dominance:

Holding onto the ball allows a team to dictate the tempo and flow of the match. By patiently circulating possession, they force the opposition to chase and react, tiring them out physically and mentally. This control translates into dominance on the field, as the team with the ball dictates where and when the game is played.

Creating Scoring Opportunities:

Possession is the foundation for creating scoring chances. By keeping the ball, teams can probe for weaknesses in the opposition's defense, create numerical overloads, and find openings for through balls or crosses. A team that can maintain possession for extended periods is more likely to create high-quality scoring chances and ultimately, score goals.

Reducing Defensive Vulnerability:

A team in possession is less likely to concede goals. By keeping the ball away from the opposition, they minimize the risk of counterattacks and limit the number of times their defense is put under pressure. This allows the team to control the game and manage the risk of conceding goals.

Psychological Impact:

Maintaining possession has a significant psychological impact on both teams. For the team in possession, it builds confidence and allows them to impose their style of play on the opposition. For the opposition, chasing the ball can be frustrating and demoralizing, leading to mistakes and a loss of focus.

Building Team Cohesion:

Possession play requires a high level of coordination and teamwork. Players need to move in sync, understand each other's movements, and make quick decisions under pressure. This constant interaction and collaboration on the field can foster a strong sense of unity and cohesion within the team.

Examples:

- **Barcelona's Tiki-Taka:** Barcelona's tiki-taka style of play, characterized by short, sharp passing and constant movement, is a prime example of the power of ball retention. Their ability to maintain possession for long periods frustrated opponents and led to numerous trophies.
- **Manchester City's Possession Dominance:** Under Pep Guardiola, Manchester City has consistently dominated possession in the Premier League. Their patient build-up play and ability to keep the ball away from opponents have been key to their success.

Ball retention is a cornerstone of modern soccer tactics. It's a strategic tool that allows teams to control the game, create scoring chances, and reduce their defensive vulnerability. While it's not the only way to win games, it has proven to be a highly effective approach for many successful teams.

CHAPTER 12: TRANSITION PLAY

Offensive Transitions

Offensive transitions, the swift and decisive shift from defense to attack, are a vital component of modern soccer tactics. They capitalize on the vulnerability of the opposition when they lose possession, turning defense into attack in the blink of an eye. Let's look into the key elements of effective offensive transitions.

Quick Reactions:

The foundation of successful offensive transitions lies in quick reactions. As soon as possession is won, players must spring into action, exploiting the disarray of the opposition's defense before they can regroup. This requires anticipation, awareness of space, and the ability to make split-second decisions.

Forward Momentum:

The initial focus of an offensive transition is to establish forward momentum. Players move the ball quickly upfield, aiming to catch the opposition off-balance and expose gaps in their defensive structure. This can be achieved through direct passes to forwards, runs into space by midfielders, or even long balls to switch the point of attack.

Exploiting Space:

Offensive transitions often expose large spaces behind the opposition's defense. Attacking players must identify and exploit these spaces, making intelligent runs in behind or positioning themselves to receive through balls. The ability to quickly recognize and utilize these opportunities can lead to dangerous goal-scoring chances.

Decision Making:

During transitions, players must make quick and intelligent decisions. They need to choose the right pass, dribble, or shot based on the situation. This requires a good understanding of the game, the ability to read the opposition's movements, and the composure to execute under pressure.

Numerical Superiority:

Offensive transitions often create situations of numerical superiority for the attacking team. When the opposition loses possession, their players are often scattered and out of position. This allows the attacking team to overload specific areas of the pitch, creating chances through combinations, crosses, or direct attacks.

Examples:

- **Liverpool's Counter-Press:** Liverpool, under Jurgen Klopp, is renowned for its aggressive counter-pressing, which triggers quick offensive transitions. They win the ball back high up the pitch and launch lightning-fast attacks.
- **Manchester City's Possession-Based Transitions:** Manchester City's possession-based style often involves quick transitions when they regain possession. Their players are trained to immediately look for forward passing options and exploit spaces left by the opposition.

Defensive Transitions

Defensive transitions are the critical moments when a team switches from attacking to defending after losing possession. These transitions are often chaotic and high-risk, as the opposition can quickly exploit the space left behind by the attacking players. Mastering defensive transitions is crucial for preventing counterattacks and maintaining defensive solidity. Let's break down the key elements of effective defensive transitions.

Immediate Reaction:

The first step in a successful defensive transition is immediate reaction. As soon as possession is lost, players must react quickly, sprinting back to their defensive positions and closing down space. This initial reaction can prevent the opposition from gaining momentum and launching a dangerous counterattack.

Regaining Shape:

The next step is to regain the team's defensive shape. This involves players returning to their designated positions, closing down passing lanes, and establishing a compact defensive block. The aim is to deny space for the opposition to operate and force them into less dangerous areas of the pitch.

Counter-Pressing:

Counter-pressing is a proactive approach to defensive transitions. Instead of simply retreating, players immediately press the opponent who has just won the ball, aiming to win it back quickly and prevent them from starting a counterattack. This requires aggression, intensity, and coordination among the players.

Delaying and Containing:

If the initial counter-press is unsuccessful, the focus shifts to delaying and containing the opposition's attack. Defenders must buy time for their teammates to recover and regain their defensive shape. This involves jockeying opponents, forcing them wide, and preventing them from making penetrating passes.

Communication:

Clear and concise communication is essential during defensive transitions. Players need to communicate with each other, providing instructions, warnings, and encouragement. This helps to maintain the defensive shape, prevent misunderstandings, and ensure everyone is on the same page.

Examples:

* **Atletico Madrid:** Diego Simeone's Atletico Madrid is renowned for their disciplined and organized defensive transitions. They quickly regain their shape after losing possession, close down space effectively, and frustrate the opposition's attempts to counterattack.
* **Manchester City:** Pep Guardiola's Manchester City excels at counter-pressing, immediately putting pressure on the opponent after losing the ball. This proactive approach often leads to regaining possession quickly in advanced areas.

Role of Key Players

Transition play in soccer, the swift shift between defense and attack, is a pivotal aspect of modern tactics. Key players emerge in these critical moments, dictating the tempo, exploiting spaces, and orchestrating decisive actions that can swing the momentum of a match. Let's look into the specific roles and contributions of key players in both offensive and defensive transitions.

Offensive Transitions:

* **The Ball-Winning Midfielder:** Often the first to pounce on a loose ball or intercept a pass, this player is the catalyst for offensive transitions. Their ability to quickly regain possession and initiate a forward move is crucial. They need to be aggressive, tenacious in the tackle, and possess excellent

ball-winning skills. Examples include N'Golo Kante (Chelsea), Casemiro (Manchester United), and Fabinho (Liverpool).

- **The Playmaker:** Once possession is secured, the playmaker takes center stage. They are the creative force, responsible for distributing the ball quickly and accurately to attackers. Their vision, passing range, and decision-making under pressure are essential for launching effective counterattacks. Think of players like Kevin De Bruyne (Manchester City), Luka Modric (Real Madrid), and Bruno Fernandes (Manchester United).
- **The Speedster:** Pacy wingers or forwards are often the primary beneficiaries of offensive transitions. Their speed allows them to exploit the space behind the opposition's defense, running onto through balls or receiving long passes to create goal-scoring opportunities. Kylian Mbappé (Paris Saint-Germain), Vinícius Júnior (Real Madrid), and Mohamed Salah (Liverpool) are prime examples of speedsters who thrive in transition.

Defensive Transitions:

- **The Defensive Midfielder:** The defensive midfielder acts as a shield for the backline during defensive transitions. They are the first line of defense, tasked with intercepting passes, tackling opponents, and slowing down the opposition's attack. Their positional awareness, anticipation, and tackling ability are crucial for preventing counterattacks. Players like Casemiro (Manchester United) and Rodri (Manchester City) excel in this role.
- **The Center-Backs:** Center-backs play a pivotal role in defensive transitions, organizing the defensive line and communicating with their teammates. They must be quick to react to turnovers, position themselves to intercept passes, and win aerial duels. Their leadership and communication skills are essential for maintaining a compact defensive shape and preventing the opposition from exploiting space. Virgil van Dijk (Liverpool), Ruben Dias (Manchester City), and Marquinhos (Paris Saint-Germain) are prime examples of modern center-backs who excel in defensive transitions.
- **The Goalkeeper:** The goalkeeper is the last line of defense and often plays a crucial role in defensive transitions. They must be alert and ready to come off their line to sweep up through balls, smother shots, or make crucial saves. Their communication and decision-making are vital for organizing the defense and preventing goals. Alisson Becker (Liverpool) and Ederson (Manchester City) are two goalkeepers who are known for their exceptional ability in defensive transitions.

Beyond Positional Roles:

While these are the primary roles involved in transition play, it's important to note that every player on the field has a role to play. Forwards need to track back and help defend, midfielders need to be aware of their defensive responsibilities, and defenders need to be able to initiate attacks. Successful transitions require a collective effort from the entire team, with each player understanding their role and executing it effectively.

CHAPTER 13: PASSING STYLES

Short Passing vs. Long Passing

Short passing and long passing are two distinct styles of play in soccer, each with its own advantages and tactical implications.

Short Passing:

Short passing involves a series of quick, precise passes between players in close proximity. It emphasizes ball retention, control of the tempo, and patient build-up play. This style of play requires players with excellent technical skills, spatial awareness, and the ability to make quick decisions under pressure.

- **Advantages:** Short passing can tire out the opposition, create numerical superiority in specific areas of the pitch, and open up passing lanes for more penetrative passes or shots. It's a style often associated with teams like Barcelona and Manchester City, who use it to dominate possession and control the game.
- **Disadvantages:** Short passing can be predictable and slow, making it difficult to break down well-organized defenses. It also requires a high level of technical ability and coordination among players.

Long Passing:

Long passing involves bypassing the opposition's midfield with direct passes to forwards or wingers. This style of play aims to quickly exploit space behind the defense and create immediate goal-scoring opportunities. It requires players with excellent passing range and accuracy, as well as forwards who can hold up the ball and bring others into play.

- **Advantages:** Long passing can catch the opposition off guard, quickly transition from defense to attack, and exploit the pace of fast attackers. It's a style often used by counter-attacking teams or those looking to break down a deep-lying defense.
- **Disadvantages:** Long passing can be risky, as inaccurate passes can easily lead to turnovers. It also requires a team to have forwards who can win aerial duels and hold up the ball effectively.

Choosing the Right Approach:

There's no one-size-fits-all answer to whether short passing or long passing is better. The most effective approach depends on the team's strengths and weaknesses, the opposition's playing style, and the specific game situation. Some teams might prefer a short-passing style when they are in control of the game, but switch to a long-passing approach when they need to chase the game or exploit a specific weakness in the opposition's defense.

The key is to have a flexible approach and be able to adapt to different situations. A team that can master both short and long passing will have a wider range of tactical options at their disposal, making them more unpredictable and difficult to defend against.

Importance of Passing Lanes

Passing lanes, the open spaces between defenders through which a player can pass the ball, are the highways of soccer tactics. They are the conduits for ball circulation, attacking progression, and ultimately, goal-scoring opportunities. Let's explore their importance and how teams utilize them to gain a tactical advantage.

Breaking Down Defenses:

Passing lanes are essential for breaking down organized defenses. When defenders are tightly packed together, passing lanes become narrow and difficult to find. However, intelligent movement off the ball by attackers and midfielders can create and exploit these lanes. A well-timed run can pull a defender out of position, opening up a passing lane for a teammate to exploit.

Maintaining Possession:

Passing lanes are crucial for maintaining possession. Teams that can quickly identify and utilize passing lanes can keep the ball moving, tiring out the opposition, and controlling the tempo of the game. By constantly offering themselves as passing options and moving into space, players create a network of passing lanes that make it difficult for the opposition to win the ball back.

Creating Attacking Opportunities:

Passing lanes are the gateways to goal-scoring opportunities. A well-timed pass through a narrow lane can put an attacker through on goal, creating a one-on-one situation with the goalkeeper. Similarly, a pass into the space behind the defense can lead to a dangerous cross or a shot on goal.

Tactical Awareness:

Identifying and exploiting passing lanes requires tactical awareness and spatial understanding. Players need to be able to read the game, anticipate their teammates' movements, and understand the positioning of the opposition's defenders. This awareness allows them to make quick decisions and exploit passing lanes before they close down.

Creating Passing Lanes:

Passing lanes can be created through various methods. Players can make runs to drag defenders out of position, use decoys to create false passing lanes, or simply position themselves in spaces where they can receive the ball. The key is to constantly offer options for the ball carrier and make it difficult for the opposition to anticipate where the pass will go.

Passing Under Pressure

Passing under pressure is a vital skill in soccer, a test of a player's technical ability, composure, and decision-making under duress. It's the art of maintaining possession and progressing play when faced with immediate pressure from the opposition.

Here's what it takes to excel at passing under pressure:

Technique:

A strong foundation in passing technique is essential. Players need a soft first touch to cushion the ball and bring it under control quickly. They need to be able to disguise their passes, using different parts of their feet to vary the direction and weight of the pass. A well-disguised pass can deceive defenders and open up passing lanes.

Awareness:

Passing under pressure demands exceptional awareness of the surrounding environment. Players need to scan the field, identify passing options, and anticipate the movement of both teammates and opponents. This awareness allows them to make quick decisions and execute the right pass under pressure.

Decision-Making:

The ability to make quick and accurate decisions is crucial. Players need to assess the situation and choose the best passing option in a split second. This involves weighing the risks and rewards of different passes, considering the positioning of teammates and opponents, and anticipating the next phase of play.

Composure:

Maintaining composure under pressure is key. Players need to stay calm and focused, even when faced with aggressive challenges from the opposition. Panicking can lead to rushed decisions and inaccurate passes. A cool head allows players to assess the situation calmly and make the right choice.

Creativity:

Sometimes, passing under pressure requires creativity. Players need to be able to improvise and find unexpected solutions to evade the press. This could involve a clever backheel, a disguised pass, or a quick one-two with a teammate.

Physical Attributes:

Passing under pressure can also be a physical battle. Players need strength and balance to shield the ball from defenders and maintain possession. They also need agility and quick feet to evade challenges and create space for themselves.

Passing as Communication

In soccer, passing is more than just moving the ball from one player to another; it's a form of non-verbal communication that conveys crucial information about the game's state, the player's intentions, and the next course of action. Let's look into the various ways a pass can communicate on the field.

Touch and Weight: The touch and weight of a pass convey immediate instructions to the receiver. A firm pass to the feet indicates "control and hold." A softer pass might signal "turn and face the play." A lofted pass suggests "use your aerial ability."

Location: The location of a pass can communicate tactical intent. A pass to the flank might mean "switch the play" or "create width." A pass through the center could signal "attack directly" or "look for a through ball." A pass back to the goalkeeper might mean "reset the attack" or "relieve pressure."

Passer and Receiver: The identity of the passer and receiver also conveys information. A pass from a defender to a midfielder might signal "build-up play," while a pass from a midfielder to a forward could mean "attacking transition." A pass between two central defenders might indicate a safe option, while a pass from a fullback to a winger could signal a more adventurous approach.

Context of the Situation: The overall context of the situation is important in interpreting the message of a pass. A pass in the defensive third might mean "maintain possession and build out," while a pass in the final third could signal "look for a goal-scoring opportunity." A pass under pressure might mean "relieve pressure," while a pass in open space could indicate "exploit the space and attack."

Examples:

- A chipped pass from a defender to an attacking midfielder's chest indicates "control the ball and turn to face forward."
- A firm pass from a midfielder to a winger's feet in the final third signals "take on your defender and create a crossing opportunity."
- A quick one-two pass between two midfielders in a central area communicates "continue the combination and break the defensive line."

By understanding the nuances of passing as communication, players can make better decisions on the field. They can anticipate their teammates' intentions, move into the right positions, and execute the appropriate actions. This improved understanding of non-verbal communication can elevate a team's performance and lead to more cohesive and effective play.

CHAPTER 14: CREATING SPACE

Movement Off the Ball

Movement off the ball is a fundamental concept in soccer tactics, as crucial as the skills displayed with the ball at one's feet. It's the art of intelligent positioning, timing, and movement without possession, aimed at creating space, manipulating defenders, and ultimately unlocking scoring opportunities.

The Art of Deception: Effective movement off the ball is a form of deception. By making runs, checking back, or simply shifting positions, players can create uncertainty in the minds of defenders. This uncertainty forces defenders to make decisions, potentially opening up spaces that can be exploited.

Creating Space for Yourself and Others: Movement off the ball is not just about individual gain. It's also about creating space for teammates. A well-timed run can drag a defender out of position, opening up a passing lane for another player. Similarly, a player dropping deep can create space for a teammate to run into behind the defense.

Types of Movement:

- **Runs in Behind:** Sprinting behind the defensive line to receive a through ball or create a goal-scoring opportunity.
- **Diagonal Runs:** Angled runs across the field to disrupt the defensive line and create passing options.
- **Checking Back:** Dropping deeper to receive the ball, dragging a defender out of position and opening up space behind them.
- **Third-Man Runs:** Arriving late in the box to receive a pass from a teammate who has played a one-two with another player.

Timing and Anticipation: The timing of movement is crucial. Making a run too early can be easily anticipated by defenders. Conversely, making a run too late might mean the opportunity has passed. The key is to anticipate the play, read your teammate's intentions, and time your run perfectly to receive the ball in a dangerous position.

Examples:

- **False Nine:** The false nine, a striker who drops deep into midfield, is a master of movement off the ball. Their movement creates space for attacking midfielders and wingers to exploit.

- **Overlapping Runs:** Fullbacks making overlapping runs past their wingers create width and attacking overloads, often catching defenders off guard.

Exploiting Defensive Weaknesses

First, you need to scout your opponents. Look for the defender who's a step slower, the one who loses focus, or the side of the field they tend to neglect. This is your target zone.

Overloads

One of the most effective ways to exploit a weakness is to create an overload. This means flooding a specific area of the field with more attackers than defenders. Let's say their right back is struggling. Send your winger and an overlapping fullback to that side. The two-on-one situation forces the defense to react, opening up gaps elsewhere.

Switching Play

If you're facing a compact defense, switching the play quickly can catch them off balance. A long diagonal pass to the opposite flank forces defenders to shift positions rapidly. If they're slow to react, a winger can exploit the space behind them.

Movement off the Ball

Sometimes the best way to create space isn't with the ball, but without it. Clever runs from your forwards and midfielders can drag defenders out of position. A striker making a diagonal run can pull a center-back out of the box, leaving space for a teammate to exploit.

The Decoy Run

A decoy run is a selfless act of tactical brilliance. One player makes a run that they know won't get them the ball, but it serves a purpose. It draws a defender away, creating space for someone else to make a more dangerous run.

The Give-and-Go

This classic move is all about quick passing and movement. A player passes the ball and immediately sprints into the space they've just vacated. If the defender follows the ball, the runner is open. If the defender follows the runner, there's space for a pass behind them.

Use of Decoys

Think of the decoy as a magician on the pitch. Their job is to create an illusion, drawing defenders away from the real threat. This opens up pockets of space that can be exploited by teammates.

Types of Decoy Runs

There are several ways to employ decoys:

- **The False 9:** A striker who drops deep, dragging a center-back out of position and leaving a gap behind for midfielders to run into.
- **The Overlapping Run:** A wide player makes a run that looks like they want the ball, pulling a defender wide and creating space in the center.
- **The Channel Run:** A forward sprints towards the corner flag, dragging a defender away from the central areas.
- **The Blindside Run:** A player sneaks in behind a defender who's focused on the ball, making them an unmarked target for a pass.

Timing is Everything

The effectiveness of a decoy run hinges on timing. The run should be made just as the ball is about to be played. This forces defenders to make split-second decisions, often leading to mistakes.

Communication is Key

Decoys aren't lone wolves. They work in tandem with their teammates. A subtle nod or a quick shout can signal a decoy run, ensuring everyone is on the same page.

The Decoy Mindset

Playing as a decoy requires selflessness and intelligence. It's not about personal glory; it's about sacrificing individual gain for the betterment of the team. A successful decoy doesn't need to touch the ball to have a massive impact on the game.

CHAPTER 15: EXPLOITING WEAKNESSES

Analyzing Opponents

Let's get down to the nitty-gritty of analyzing your opponents in soccer. This isn't just about knowing their names and jersey numbers; it's about understanding their tendencies, weaknesses, and how you can exploit them.

Scouting: Your Secret Weapon

Scouting is like having a cheat code for the game. Watch footage of their previous matches. Look for patterns in their play:

- **Defensive Weaknesses:** Does a fullback get caught out of position? Do they struggle with crosses? Is there a specific side they favor?
- **Offensive Tendencies:** Do they rely on long balls or build up from the back? Which player is their main creative outlet?
- **Set Pieces:** Are they vulnerable to corners or free kicks? Do they have a particular player who's a threat in the air?

Reading the Game in Real Time

Once the match starts, pay attention to how your opponents react under pressure.

- **Individual Errors:** Do they give away the ball easily? Are they prone to mistimed tackles?
- **Collective Weaknesses:** Does their defense leave gaps when they push forward? Do they struggle to track runners?
- **Tactical Adjustments:** Do they change their formation or approach based on the score or time remaining?

Adapting Your Game Plan

Once you've identified weaknesses, it's time to adjust your tactics.

- **Exploiting Space:** If a fullback is often out of position, overload that side of the field with attackers.
- **Pressuring Weaknesses:** If a player is prone to losing the ball, apply targeted pressure to force them into mistakes.
- **Playing to Your Strengths:** If your team excels at counter-attacks and your opponent struggles with defending them, look for opportunities to hit them on the break.

The Importance of Flexibility

Remember, soccer is a dynamic game. Your opponents might adapt to your tactics, so be prepared to adjust on the fly. Keep a close eye on the game and communicate with your teammates to exploit new weaknesses as they arise.

Targeting Specific Players or Areas

Scouting is your first step. You need to identify the weak links in your opponent's chain. Is their left-back prone to rash challenges? Does a midfielder give away the ball often? Is there a specific zone they struggle to defend?

The Isolated Defender

If you find a defender who's consistently isolated, exploit it. Create overloads by sending two or three attackers at them. The defender will be outnumbered and forced to make quick decisions, often resulting in mistakes.

The Slow Center Back

Got a center-back who lacks pace? Look for opportunities to play balls over the top for your fast forwards to run onto. Their speed can expose the defender's weakness and create scoring chances.

The Aerial Vulnerability

If a team struggles to defend crosses, target their weakness. Get the ball out wide and whip in deliveries into the box. Your taller players can win aerial duels and create chaos in the penalty area.

The Playmaker

Sometimes, the key to unlocking a defense is by neutralizing their playmaker. Apply high pressure when they receive the ball, forcing them to rush their decisions or make errors. If they can't dictate the tempo, the whole team suffers.

The Weak Side

Every team has a weaker side, whether it's due to individual shortcomings or tactical preferences. Identify their weak side and focus your attacks there. You'll create a numerical advantage, putting their defense under constant pressure.

Adapt and Evolve

Your opponent isn't static. They may adjust their tactics to counter your approach.

There's a bit of a meta game component to it – they know that you know that they know, etc.

Your opponents will know what their weaknesses are just as you know yours and know how your opponent is likely to exploit them, which affects how you choose your tactics, which affects theirs, and so on.

Stay alert, adapt your game plan, and look for new ways to exploit their weaknesses as the game progresses.

Adjusting Tactics Accordingly

You can't enter a match with a rigid game plan. Soccer is fluid, and your opponent will adapt, forcing you to adjust. Think of yourself as a chess player, anticipating their moves and making calculated responses.

Pressing High or Sitting Back

If your opponent has a shaky defense, a high press can force turnovers in dangerous areas. But if they're skilled at playing out from the back, sitting back and absorbing pressure might be a smarter choice.

Width or Narrowness

If their fullbacks are adventurous, exploit the space they leave behind by spreading the play wide. But if they have a narrow defensive line, focus your attacks centrally to overload their midfield.

Direct or Possession-Based

If their defense struggles with long balls, don't be afraid to go direct. But if they're well-organized and compact, a patient possession game can create openings as they tire.

Man Marking or Zonal Defense

If they have a star player who's the heart of their attack, consider man-marking them. But if they have a well-balanced attack, a zonal defense might be more effective in maintaining your shape.

In-Game Adjustments

Don't wait until halftime to make changes. If your initial tactics aren't working, be proactive. Switch formations, change your attacking patterns, or adjust your defensive positioning.

The Coach's Role

The coach plays a crucial role in tactical adjustments. They have a bird's-eye view of the game and can spot patterns that players might miss. They can also communicate instructions to the team more effectively.

The Players' Responsibility

While the coach sets the overall strategy, players must be adaptable and intelligent on the pitch. They need to read the game, understand the adjustments, and execute them effectively.

CHAPTER 16: SET PIECES AND DEAD BALL SITUATIONS

Free Kicks: Direct vs. Indirect

Let's break down the difference between direct and indirect free kicks in soccer. These dead ball situations can be game-changers, so understanding the nuances is crucial.

Direct Free Kicks: Aim for Glory

A direct free kick is your golden ticket to score directly. If you strike the ball cleanly and it sails past the goalkeeper into the net, it's a goal. No need for anyone else to touch it.

When are Direct Free Kicks Awarded?

These are usually given for more serious fouls:

- **Fouls:** Tripping, kicking, pushing, or reckless challenges.
- **Handballs:** Deliberately handling the ball.

Tactical Options:

- **Direct Shot:** If you're close enough, go for goal!
- **Curling Effort:** Bend it around the wall and into the top corner.
- **Low Drive:** Power it under the jumping wall or through a gap.
- **Set Play:** Create a choreographed routine with your teammates to confuse the defense and open up space.

Indirect Free Kicks: Teamwork Makes the Dream Work

An indirect free kick requires a bit more teamwork. You can't score directly from it. The ball must be touched by another player (from either team) before it crosses the goal line.

When are Indirect Free Kicks Awarded?

These are typically for less serious offenses:

- **Offside:** Being in an illegal position when the ball is played.
- **Dangerous Play:** High kicks or playing in a reckless manner.

- **Obstruction:** Impeding an opponent's movement without making contact.

Tactical Options:

- **Lay-Off:** Pass it to a teammate for a shot.
- **Chip to the Back Post:** Loft the ball for an attacker to head home.
- **Dummy Run:** Create confusion by having a player pretend to take the kick, then have another player surprise the defense.

Referee Signals

How do you tell the difference between a direct and indirect free kick? The referee signals:

- **Direct Free Kick:** Points their arm towards the goal.
- **Indirect Free Kick:** Raises their arm straight up in the air until the ball is touched by another player.

Corners and Throw-Ins

These might seem like simple restarts, but they're goldmines for tactical opportunities in soccer.

Corners: The Aerial Assault

A corner kick is basically a free hit from the corner of the field. It's a chance to launch the ball into a dangerous area, creating chaos and potential scoring opportunities.

Attacking Options:

- **Inswinging or Outswinging:** Curve the ball towards or away from the goal, forcing defenders to react differently.
- **Near or Far Post:** Aim for the near post to create a quick flick-on, or the far post for a header at goal.
- **Short Corner:** Pass the ball to a teammate near the corner flag to create new angles and outmaneuver the defense.
- **Set Plays:** Practice choreographed routines with your teammates to catch the opposition off guard.

Defensive Strategies:

- **Zonal Marking:** Assign players to specific zones in the box to defend.
- **Man-to-Man Marking:** Each defender tracks a specific attacker.
- **Hybrid Marking:** Combine zonal and man-to-man marking.
- **Clearing the Lines:** Focus on getting the ball away from the danger zone as quickly as possible.

Throw-Ins: The Hidden Weapon

Don't underestimate the power of a throw-in. It's a chance to maintain possession, restart play quickly, or even create a scoring opportunity.

Tactical Uses:

- **Quick Throw:** Catch the defense off guard by throwing the ball quickly to a teammate.
- **Long Throw:** Launch the ball into the box like a cross, creating aerial challenges for your attackers.
- **Short Throw:** Maintain possession and build up play from the back.
- **Throw-In to Feet:** Pass the ball to a teammate's feet for a controlled restart.

Defending Throw-Ins:

- **Pressure:** Don't let the thrower have an easy pass. Close them down quickly to force a mistake.
- **Mark Tight:** Track the player receiving the throw-in to prevent them from turning and attacking.
- **Deny Space:** Cut off passing lanes and force the thrower to make a difficult decision.

Overall, corners and throw-ins are more than just restarts. They're tactical weapons that can swing momentum in your favor.

Penalty Strategies

Penalties aren't just about luck (though that plays a role). There are strategies and tactics involved that can significantly increase your chances of success.

For the Penalty Taker:

- **Pick Your Spot:** Before you even approach the ball, decide where you're going to shoot. Don't change your mind at the last moment.

- **Power or Placement:** A powerful shot can be unstoppable, but a well-placed shot is harder to anticipate. Choose your weapon wisely.
- **Keep Your Cool:** Penalties are a mental game. Stay calm, focus on your technique, and don't let the pressure get to you.
- **The Stutter Step:** Some players use a stutter step or a little pause in their run-up to try and throw off the goalkeeper. Use it sparingly and only if it's part of your natural technique.
- **Mix It Up:** Don't become predictable. If you always shoot to the same side, the goalkeeper will eventually figure it out.

For the Goalkeeper:

- **Do Your Homework:** Study the penalty takers. Do they have a preferred side? Any tells in their run-up?
- **Stay Big:** Make yourself as large as possible in the goal. The more space you cover, the less likely the shooter is to find a gap.
- **Choose Your Moment:** You don't have to dive early. Wait for the shooter to commit, then react.
- **Use Your Feet:** If the shot is low, don't be afraid to use your feet to make the save.
- **The Mind Games:** A little gamesmanship can go a long way. Try staring down the shooter or delaying your set position.

The Penalty Shootout:

- **Order Matters:** Choose your penalty takers wisely. Start with your most confident players to build momentum.
- **Sudden Death:** In sudden death, the pressure intensifies. Stay calm and focused.
- **Goalkeeper's Advantage:** Goalkeepers have a slight advantage in penalty shootouts due to the pressure on the takers.

Penalties are a battle of nerves as much as they are a test of skill. By understanding the strategies involved and preparing mentally, you can increase your chances of emerging victorious from the spot.

CHAPTER 17: TECHNOLOGY IN TACTICAL PLANNING

Use of Data Analytics

Gone are the days of relying solely on gut feeling and anecdotal evidence. Data analytics provides coaches and analysts with a treasure trove of information:

- **Player Tracking:** GPS and camera systems track every movement of every player, revealing distances covered, sprints, and heatmaps. This helps identify work rates, fitness levels, and tactical positioning.
- **Event Data:** Detailed logs of every pass, shot, tackle, and dribble. This allows analysts to assess passing accuracy, shot efficiency, defensive contributions, and individual player tendencies.
- **Opponent Analysis:** By studying an opponent's data, teams can identify patterns in their play, predict their strategies, and exploit weaknesses.

The Tactical Advantage

Data analytics transforms this raw information into actionable insights:

- **Formation Optimization:** Identify which formations and lineups yield the best results based on statistical analysis.
- **Tactical Tweaks:** Pinpoint areas of improvement, such as adjusting passing patterns or defensive positioning.
- **Player Development:** Tailor training programs to individual player needs based on performance data.
- **Recruitment:** Identify potential signings by analyzing player data from lower leagues or other competitions.

Beyond the Numbers

While data analytics is a powerful tool, it's important to remember that soccer isn't just about numbers. Human intuition, experience, and creativity still have a big part. The best teams use data to inform their decisions, not dictate them.

The Future of Soccer Tactics

As technology advances, we can expect even more sophisticated data analytics tools. Machine learning algorithms will uncover hidden patterns, virtual reality simulations will help teams visualize tactical scenarios, and wearable devices will track even more detailed player metrics.

Video Analysis Tools

Modern video analysis tools do more than just show you the game again. They offer a toolbox to turn raw footage into tactical gold:

- **Telestration:** Draw directly on the screen to highlight player runs, passing lanes, and tactical formations. This makes communication between coaches and players incredibly clear and focused.
- **Tagging and Coding:** Categorize specific actions like passes, shots, tackles, and set pieces. This leads to deep statistical analysis, revealing trends and tendencies that can be exploited.
- **Multiple Angles:** See the game from different viewpoints to gain a complete picture of what's happening on the pitch.
- **Slow Motion and Zoom:** Break down complex plays frame-by-frame to analyze player technique, decisions, and movement patterns.

Pre-Game Prep: The Scouting Advantage

Video analysis tools are a secret weapon for scouting opponents:

- **Spot Weak Links:** Find patterns in their defensive shape, track individual player habits, and uncover vulnerabilities in set pieces.
- **Craft Counter-Tactics:** Tailor your game plan to expose their weaknesses. Maybe you press high, target a specific player, or focus on exploiting their set pieces.
- **Prep Your Players:** Give your team a visual breakdown of the opponent's style. Provide specific instructions on how to neutralize their threats.

Post-Game Review: Lessons Learned

Video analysis isn't just for pre-game homework. It's a powerful tool for analyzing past performance:

- **Review and Improve:** Identify what worked and what didn't. Look for tactical mistakes, missed opportunities, and areas for improvement.
- **Individual Feedback:** Give players personalized clips highlighting their strengths and weaknesses, along with tips for improvement.
- **Tactical Evolution:** Track your team's progress over time and tweak your tactics as needed.

Leveling the Playing Field

Video analysis tools aren't just for the pros anymore. Affordable and easy-to-use software is now available for teams at all levels. This means everyone has access to the kind of insights that were once exclusive to top clubs.

GPS and Wearable Technology

Think of GPS trackers as a player's digital footprint on the pitch. These small devices, often worn in vests or tucked into pockets, record a wealth of data:

- **Distance Covered:** Not just the total distance, but also the intensity of movements like walking, jogging, sprinting, and high-intensity runs.
- **Speed and Acceleration:** Track a player's top speed and how quickly they reach it, revealing their explosiveness and ability to create separation.
- **Heatmaps:** Visual representations of where a player spends most of their time on the field, highlighting areas of influence and potential tactical adjustments.
- **Workload and Fatigue:** Monitor heart rate, exertion levels, and recovery time to prevent injuries and optimize training programs.

From Data to Decisions

This mountain of data is useless without analysis. Coaches and analysts use specialized software to translate raw numbers into actionable insights:

- **Tactical Assessment:** Evaluate player positioning, movement patterns, and overall team shape. Identify strengths and weaknesses in your tactics and make data-driven adjustments.
- **Individual Player Performance:** Compare individual player data to team averages and identify areas for improvement. Tailor training sessions to address specific needs.
- **Load Management:** Monitor player workloads to ensure they're not being overworked, reducing the risk of injuries.

Wearable Tech: Beyond GPS

GPS is just the tip of the iceberg. Wearable technology in soccer also includes:

- **Heart Rate Monitors:** Measure heart rate variability to assess fatigue and stress levels, allowing for personalized training plans and recovery strategies.
- **Impact Sensors:** Track the intensity of collisions and impacts to identify potential injury risks and monitor recovery.

CHAPTER 18: CHANGING TACTICS DURING A GAME

Recognizing the Need for Change

Let's talk about the art of recognizing when to change tactics during a soccer match. This is a crucial skill, as sticking to a failing plan can be disastrous.

The Scoreboard Isn't Everything

While the score is a key indicator, it's not the sole factor in deciding whether to change tactics. You need to analyze the game's flow, identify patterns, and understand why your initial plan isn't working.

Signs Your Tactics Are Failing

Here are some red flags that might signal a need for change:

- **Conceding Goals:** If you're leaking goals, especially from similar patterns of play, your defensive structure might be flawed.
- **Struggling to Create Chances:** If your attack is toothless and you're not generating shots, your offensive approach might need tweaking.
- **Losing the Midfield Battle:** If your opponent dominates possession and controls the tempo, your midfield might be outnumbered or outplayed.
- **Individual Struggles:** If key players are having an off day or are being nullified by their opponents, tactical adjustments might be necessary to get them back in the game.
- **Your Opponent's Changes:** If your opponent has made successful tactical changes, you need to adapt or risk being outmaneuvered.

Trust Your Instincts

Sometimes, the need for change isn't obvious from the stats or the scoreboard. It's a gut feeling, a sense that something isn't clicking. Trust your instincts and be prepared to make bold decisions.

The Halftime Huddle

Halftime is a crucial opportunity to reassess and adjust. Gather feedback from your players, analyze the first half, and come up with a plan for the second half.

In-Game Adjustments

Don't wait until halftime to make changes. If you spot a problem early on, don't be afraid to make a tactical switch during the game. The earlier you react, the more time you have to turn things around.

Communication is Key

When making tactical changes, communication is essential. Clearly explain your new plan to your players, ensuring everyone understands their roles and responsibilities.

The Art of Flexibility

Successful coaches and teams are adaptable. They don't cling to a predetermined plan if it's not working. They're willing to experiment, try new things, and embrace the ever-changing nature of the game.

Making Effective Substitutions

Don't wait until your team is desperate or a player is injured. Substitutions should be proactive, not reactive. Look for opportunities to inject fresh energy, change the tempo, or exploit a weakness in the opponent's game.

Matching the Needs of the Game

Consider the specific situation on the pitch:

- **Chasing the Game:** If you're behind, bring on attacking players to bolster your offense. A speedy winger or a clinical finisher can turn the tide.
- **Protecting a Lead:** If you're ahead, consider defensive reinforcements to solidify your backline. A fresh fullback or a disciplined holding midfielder can help you see out the victory.
- **Tactical Shift:** If your initial game plan isn't working, change the formation or system by introducing players with different skill sets.
- **Fatigue:** If key players are tiring, don't hesitate to replace them with fresh legs. A burst of energy can be the difference maker.
- **Injury:** If a player is injured, assess the severity and decide whether a substitution is necessary. Sometimes, a quick patch-up is enough.

The Right Player for the Right Job

Choose your substitutes wisely. Each player brings unique qualities to the table:

- **Impact Substitutes:** These players are game-changers. They bring a spark, a moment of magic, or a tactical shift that can unlock a stubborn defense.
- **Tactical Substitutes:** These players are chosen to fulfill a specific role, like adding defensive stability or providing width in attack.
- **Utility Players:** Versatile players who can play multiple positions are invaluable. They offer flexibility and allow for mid-game adjustments.

Communicate Clearly

Make sure your substitutes understand their role before they step onto the pitch. Clearly communicate your expectations, tactical instructions, and any specific tasks they need to perform.

Manage Expectations

Not every substitution will be a success. Sometimes, it takes time for a substitute to integrate into the game. Be patient and trust your decision-making.

Tactical Adjustments

This is where the real chess match unfolds, where coaches and players adapt on the fly to gain an edge over their opponents.

The Balancing Act: Offense vs. Defense

It's a constant tug-of-war. Do you push forward in search of goals, or do you prioritize defensive solidity? The answer isn't always straightforward. It depends on the scoreline, the opponent, and the overall game situation.

- **When You're Behind:** If you're trailing, you'll need to take more risks and commit more players forward. This might mean pushing your full-backs higher, playing more quickly, substituting in offense-focused players like strikers and attacking midfielders, playing with a higher defensive line, or switching to a more attacking formation.
- **When You're Ahead:** If you have the lead, you can afford to be more conservative. Drop deeper, compact the space between the lines, play slower, and focus on protecting your goal.
- **Evenly Matched:** In a closely contested game, the balance between offense and defense is crucial. Look for opportunities to counter-attack when your opponent is vulnerable, but also be prepared to defend resolutely when they come at you.

Know Thy Enemy: Opponent Strengths and Weaknesses

Before the match, you've analyzed your opponent's strengths and weaknesses. Now, it's time to apply that knowledge in real-time.

- **Exploit Weaknesses:** If their right-back is prone to getting caught out of position, overload that side of the field with your attackers. If their midfield is slow to react, hit them with quick counter-attacks.
- **Neutralize Strengths:** If their striker is a physical powerhouse, have your defenders mark them tightly and deny them space. If they have a playmaker who dictates the tempo, apply high pressure and disrupt their rhythm.

The Scoreboard: A Tactical Compass

The scoreline is a powerful influencer of tactical decisions:

- **Early Lead:** If you score an early goal, you can afford to sit back and absorb pressure, inviting your opponent to attack and leave gaps for you to exploit on the counter.
- **Late Deficit:** If you're behind in the dying minutes, throw caution to the wind. Push everyone forward, gamble on set pieces, and try everything you can to salvage a point.
- **Close Game:** In a tight match, the score can change the entire complexion of the game. A single goal can prompt a shift in mentality and tactics for both teams.

The Mental Game: Adapting to Circumstances

Tactical adjustments aren't just about X's and O's on a whiteboard. They're also about psychology and momentum.

- **Frustrated Opponent:** If your opponent is growing frustrated with your tactics, stick with them. Keep them guessing and don't give them an easy way back into the game.
- **Momentum Shift:** If the momentum of the game suddenly swings in your opponent's favor, make a change to disrupt their rhythm. A tactical substitution or a shift in formation can help you regain control.

CHAPTER 19: OPPONENT ANALYSIS AND SCOUTING

Pre-Match Analysis

This is where the tactical groundwork is laid, before a single whistle blows. It's about gaining an edge by understanding your opponent inside and out.

Scouting: Beyond the Basics

We're not just talking about knowing their star players and usual formation. Dig deeper:

- **Playing Style:** Do they favor possession or a direct approach? Are they aggressive or more conservative? Do they build up play from the back or rely on long balls?
- **Formations:** What formations do they typically use? How do they adjust based on the opponent or game situation? Look for patterns in their shape and player positioning.
- **Strengths:** Where do they excel? Do they have a clinical finisher? A dominant midfielder? A rock-solid defense?
- **Weaknesses:** Every team has them. Do they struggle with defending set pieces? Are their fullbacks vulnerable to pace? Does their goalkeeper have a tendency to spill shots?
- **Key Players:** Identify their most influential players. Who's the playmaker? Who's the defensive anchor? Who's the set-piece specialist?

Sources of Information:

- **Match Footage:** Watch recent games, ideally against similar opponents to you. Look for patterns in their play, both offensively and defensively.
- **Statistics:** Dive into the numbers. Analyze their possession stats, passing accuracy, shots on goal, defensive actions, and any other relevant metrics.
- **Opponent Interviews:** If available, listen to what their players and coaches say about their own team and their approach to the upcoming match.
- **Scout Reports:** Consult professional scouts or analysts for detailed breakdowns of the opponent's tactics and individual players.

Game Plan Development

Based on your analysis, start crafting a game plan:

- **Exploit Weaknesses:** If you've identified a weakness in their defense, design your attack to target that area.
- **Neutralize Strengths:** Develop strategies to limit their most dangerous players and disrupt their preferred style of play.
- **Play to Your Strengths:** Identify your team's strengths and design tactics that maximize your chances of success.

Pre-match analysis is an ongoing process that continues even as the game unfolds. Be prepared to adjust your tactics based on what you see on the pitch. But with thorough preparation, you'll enter the match with a clear plan, a deeper understanding of your opponent, and a significant advantage in the tactical battle.

How to Choose Tactics Based on Opponent

This is where your pre-match analysis really pays off.

It's Like a Game of Rock-Paper-Scissors

Think of soccer tactics like a game of rock-paper-scissors, with each style having its own strengths and weaknesses.

- **Opponent Loves Possession?** Don't try to out-possess them. Instead, focus on disrupting their rhythm with high pressure or dropping back into a compact defensive block and hitting them on the counter-attack.
- **They Play Direct?** Don't get sucked into their long-ball game. Instead, try to control possession, play through midfield, and exploit the space behind their defense with quick passing and movement.
- **They're Known for High Pressing?** Don't panic on the ball. Stay calm, play quick passes, and look for opportunities to exploit the space behind their high line.

Exploit Their Weaknesses

Remember that scouting report you put together? Now's the time to use it.

- **Weak Fullbacks?** Attack their flanks with pace and width.
- **Slow Center Backs?** Play balls over the top for your speedy forwards.
- **Vulnerable to Set Pieces?** Focus on creating corners and free kicks in dangerous areas.

Play to Your Strengths

Choosing tactics isn't just about countering your opponent. It's also about maximizing your own strengths.

- **Got a Dominant Midfield?** Control possession and dictate the tempo.
- **Fast Forwards?** Hit them on the counter-attack.
- **Solid Defense?** Soak up pressure and frustrate your opponents.

Be Adaptable

No game plan is foolproof. Your opponent might surprise you with a tactical change or a formation you didn't expect. Be prepared to adjust your tactics mid-game to counter their adjustments.

Choosing the right tactics is a bit like solving a puzzle. You need to consider your opponent's strengths and weaknesses, your own team's capabilities, and the ever-changing dynamics of the game.

In-Game Observations

Think of the game as a chessboard, constantly shifting and evolving. Your pre-match analysis is your opening move, but the game truly begins when the whistle blows.

Eyes on the Prize: Key Observations

Here's what to look for:

- **Formation and Shape:** How is the opponent setting up? Are they playing with a high line or a deep block? Are they compact or leaving gaps?
- **Player Movement:** How are their players moving on and off the ball? Are they making overlapping runs? Who's dropping deep to receive the ball?
- **Passing Patterns:** How are they building their attacks? Are they playing through the midfield or going long? Are they targeting specific areas of the pitch?
- **Defensive Weaknesses:** Are they struggling to track runners? Are they leaving space behind the full-backs? Are they vulnerable to counter-attacks?
- **Individual Player Tendencies:** Does their striker tend to drift wide? Does their goalkeeper rush off their line? Does their playmaker always cut inside on their favored foot?

Reading Between the Lines

Don't just observe what's happening; try to understand why.

- **Why are they playing a particular formation?** Are they trying to control possession? Are they trying to expose a weakness in your team?
- **Why are they targeting a specific area of the pitch?** Do they see a vulnerability in your defense? Are they trying to exploit a matchup advantage?
- **Why are they making certain substitutions?** Are they trying to change the game's tempo? Are they trying to shore up their defense or add more attacking threat?

Real-Time Adjustments

Based on your observations, make tactical adjustments on the fly.

- **Change Formation:** If your initial formation isn't working, switch to a different shape.
- **Adjust Player Roles:** Give your players specific instructions based on what you see happening on the field.
- **Exploit Weaknesses:** If you spot a vulnerability in the opponent's defense, adjust your attack to exploit it.

Post-Match Review

This is where the real learning happens, where you dissect the game to understand what went right, what went wrong, and how you can improve.

It's Not Just About the Result

Whether you won, lost, or drew, every match is a learning opportunity. Don't get caught up in the emotions of the result. Instead, focus on the tactical details and how you can evolve as a team.

The Film Room: Your Tactical Classroom

Gather your team (and coaching staff, if you have one) and rewatch the game footage. This is your chance to:

- **Analyze Your Tactics:** Did your game plan work as intended? Did you successfully exploit the opponent's weaknesses? Did your players execute your instructions effectively?
- **Identify Errors:** Pinpoint mistakes in positioning, decision-making, and execution. Was there a defensive lapse that led to a goal? Did a missed pass cost you a scoring chance?

- **Assess Individual Performances:** Evaluate each player's contribution. Who stood out? Who struggled? What areas do they need to improve on?
- **Learn from the Opposition:** How did your opponent counter your tactics? What did they do well that you could learn from?
- **Data Deep Dive:** If you have access to match statistics and tracking data, use it to supplement your video analysis. This can provide valuable insights into areas like possession, passing accuracy, and defensive actions.

Honest Feedback is Key

Encourage an open and honest discussion during the review. Players should feel comfortable sharing their perspectives and offering constructive criticism.

Turn Insights into Action

Don't let the post-match review become just another meeting. The insights gained should directly inform your future training sessions and game plans.

- **Tactical Tweaks:** If you identified weaknesses in your tactics, adjust your approach for the next match.
- **Individual Training:** If certain players struggled, provide them with personalized training drills to address their weaknesses.
- **Team Drills:** Use training sessions to practice specific tactical scenarios that arose during the match.

CHAPTER 20: TACTICAL PERIODIZATION

Planning the Season

Let's talk about planning your season with tactical periodization. This isn't just about scheduling practices; it's about strategically mapping out your tactical development throughout the year.

Divide and Conquer: The Macrocycle

Break your season into distinct phases or cycles:

- **Pre-Season:** This is your foundation-building phase. Focus on fitness, conditioning, and introducing the core tactical principles of your game model.
- **Early Season:** As the competitive matches begin, you can fine-tune your tactics and address specific weaknesses exposed in early games.
- **Mid-Season:** This is where you maintain your tactical edge and introduce variations to your game model to keep opponents guessing.
- **Late Season:** If you're in contention for trophies, this is the time to peak tactically. Refine your strategies, focus on set pieces, and ensure your players are mentally prepared for the crucial matches.

Each Phase Has Its Own Focus

Don't try to cram everything into one phase. Each cycle should have a clear tactical focus:

- **Pre-Season:** Master the basics of your formation, build defensive solidity, and establish your preferred attacking patterns.
- **Early Season:** Experiment with different tactical variations, test your players' understanding of the game model, and adapt to the strengths and weaknesses of specific opponents.
- **Mid-Season:** Introduce more complex tactical concepts, work on transitions between defense and attack, and develop your set-piece routines.
- **Late Season:** Fine-tune your tactics for specific opponents, focus on mental preparation, and ensure your players are physically and mentally fresh for the decisive matches.

Don't Forget the Microcycles

Within each phase, break down your training into weekly or even daily microcycles. These microcycles should include a variety of training sessions focusing on different tactical aspects:

- **Tactical Drills:** Practice specific game situations, like defensive transitions or attacking in wide areas.
- **Video Analysis:** Review game footage to identify tactical strengths and weaknesses and to reinforce learning.
- **Theoretical Sessions:** Hold discussions with players to clarify tactical concepts and strategies.

Balancing Training Loads

This isn't just about avoiding burnout; it's about optimizing performance throughout the season.

The Goldilocks Zone: Not Too Much, Not Too Little

Think of training load like a porridge bowl: too much, and you burn out; too little, and you don't progress. The goal is to find the sweet spot where you challenge your players without overloading them.

Monitoring the Load

Keep a close eye on both internal and external load:

- **Internal Load:** This is the physiological and psychological stress on the player. Monitor heart rate, perceived exertion, and sleep quality.
- **External Load:** This is the physical workload, measured in distance covered, sprints, high-intensity actions, and training volume.

Peaking at the Right Time

Don't train at maximum intensity all the time. Periodize your training to peak for key matches:

- **Early Season:** Build a solid foundation with a focus on aerobic fitness and basic tactical principles. Gradually increase the intensity.
- **Mid-Season:** Maintain fitness levels while refining tactical details. Introduce variations and game-specific scenarios.
- **Late Season:** Taper off the training load to ensure players are fresh and peaking physically and mentally for crucial matches.

Listen to Your Players' Bodies

Every player is different. Pay attention to individual responses to training. Some players might recover quickly, while others might need more time. Tailor training loads accordingly.

Rest and Recovery are Essential

Don't neglect rest and recovery. It's during rest periods that the body adapts and grows stronger. Include adequate sleep, proper nutrition, and active recovery techniques like stretching and massage.

Adjusting the Plan

Be prepared to modify your training plan based on:

*   **Fixture Congestion:** If you have a busy schedule, reduce the training load to avoid overtraining.
*   **Injuries:** Adjust training loads for injured players to ensure a safe and effective recovery.
*   **Performance:** If a player is struggling, it might be a sign of fatigue. Give them extra rest or reduce their workload.

Tactical Drills and Exercises

This is where you translate theory into practice, where your team's tactical understanding comes to life on the training ground.

Game-Realistic Scenarios: Bridge the Gap

Don't just have your players run laps and do isolated drills. Create game-realistic scenarios that simulate the challenges they'll face in a match.

*   **Small-Sided Games:** Divide the squad into smaller teams and play on a reduced pitch. This forces quicker decision-making, tighter spaces, and increased intensity.
*   **Possession Drills:** Focus on maintaining possession under pressure, working on passing triangles, and exploiting numerical advantages.
*   **Transition Drills:** Practice switching quickly between defense and attack, emphasizing counter-pressing and fast breaks.
*   **Set-Piece Routines:** Choreograph corners, free kicks, and throw-ins to create scoring opportunities.

Targeted Training: Address Specific Weaknesses

Identify areas where your team needs improvement and design drills to address those specific weaknesses.

- **Defensive Shape:** Use drills that focus on maintaining a compact shape, tracking runners, and communicating effectively.
- **Attacking Patterns:** Practice combination play, overlapping runs, and exploiting space behind the defense.
- **Set-Piece Defense:** Drill zonal marking, man-to-man marking, and clearing the ball from danger zones.

Progression and Variation

Don't let your drills become stale. Start with simple exercises and gradually increase the complexity:

- **Add Defenders:** Start with a basic attacking drill and gradually add defenders to create a more realistic challenge.
- **Introduce Constraints:** Limit touches, restrict space, or impose time limits to force players to think and react quickly.
- **Vary the Conditions:** Change the size of the pitch, the number of players, or the specific tactical focus of the drill to keep things fresh and engaging.

The Coach's Role: Guide and Correct

The coach is the architect of tactical drills. They design the exercises, set the objectives, and provide feedback to players.

- **Clear Instructions:** Explain the purpose of the drill and the specific tactical principles you want to reinforce.
- **Active Observation:** Watch the drill closely, identify areas for improvement, and offer constructive criticism.
- **Individual Attention:** Provide personalized feedback to each player, highlighting their strengths and areas where they can improve.

Tactical drills are an essential part of your team's development. By creating realistic scenarios, targeting specific weaknesses, and providing clear guidance, you can equip your players with the tactical tools they need to succeed on game day.

CHAPTER 21: MAN MARKING VS. ZONAL MARKING

Principles of Man Marking

Man-marking is simple in concept: each defender is assigned a specific opponent to mark. It's like having a personal bodyguard, following your assigned player wherever they go on the pitch.

Key Principles:

- **Stick Tight:** Maintain close proximity to your assigned player, denying them space and time on the ball.
- **Body Positioning:** Position yourself between the player and the goal, cutting off passing lanes and forcing them away from dangerous areas.
- **Communication:** Talk to your teammates to ensure there are no overlaps or gaps in coverage.
- **Anticipation:** Read your opponent's movement and anticipate their next move. This allows you to react quickly and intercept passes or block shots.
- **Physicality:** Man-marking often requires physicality and aggression. Be prepared to challenge for the ball and make tackles.

When to Employ Man-Marking

Man-marking is most effective in specific situations:

- **Neutralizing a Star Player:** If the opponent has a standout player who poses a significant threat, man-marking can take them out of the game.
- **Set Pieces:** Man-marking is often used on corners and free kicks to prevent specific players from getting free headers or shots.
- **Tactical Flexibility:** Man-marking can be used as a surprise tactic to disrupt an opponent's rhythm or exploit a specific weakness.

The Risks and Rewards

Man-marking isn't without its drawbacks:

- **Space Behind:** If your defenders follow their assigned players too far, it can leave gaps in your defensive line that the opposition can exploit.
- **Fatigue:** Man-marking can be physically demanding, especially if you're chasing a quick or elusive opponent.
- **Tactical Vulnerability:** If the opponent is adept at switching play or using decoy runs, man-marking can be easily exploited.

Ultimately, the decision of whether to use man-marking depends on your team's strengths, your opponent's weaknesses, and the specific game situation. It's a tactical tool that, when used effectively, can disrupt the opposition's flow and neutralize their key players. However, it requires discipline, communication, and a willingness to adapt if the situation demands it.

Advantages and Disadvantages of Zonal Marking

This defensive approach is all about defending spaces rather than specific players, like guarding a territory instead of chasing a shadow.

Advantages of Zonal Marking:

- **Maintains Shape:** Zonal marking helps your team maintain a compact and organized defensive structure. This makes it harder for opponents to find gaps and penetrate your lines.
- **Covers Passing Lanes:** By focusing on zones, you can effectively block passing lanes and force opponents to play predictable passes.
- **Collective Responsibility:** Zonal marking promotes teamwork and communication. Defenders work together to cover their assigned areas and ensure no one is left unmarked.
- **Conserves Energy:** Compared to man-marking, zonal marking can be less physically demanding, as defenders don't have to constantly chase opponents around the field.
- **Adaptability:** Zonal marking allows you to adjust to different attacking formations and player movements more easily than man-marking.

Disadvantages of Zonal Marking:

- **Marking Gaps:** If a player moves between zones or on the boundary of two zones, it can create confusion and leave space for opponents to exploit.
- **Aerial Challenges:** Zonal marking can be vulnerable to aerial attacks, as defenders might struggle to win headers against taller opponents.
- **Lack of Pressure on the Ball:** Zonal marking often results in less immediate pressure on the ball carrier, giving them more time and space to make decisions.
- **Requires Tactical Discipline:** Zonal marking demands a high level of tactical awareness and communication from defenders to ensure effective coverage and prevent gaps from opening up.
- **Vulnerable to Overloads:** If the opponent floods a specific zone with attackers, it can overwhelm the defenders in that area.

When to Use Zonal Marking:

Zonal marking is often preferred when facing teams with fluid attacking movements and good off-the-ball runs. It's also useful when you have a technically sound defense that excels at communication and positional awareness.

Hybrid Systems

Hybrid marking systems in soccer is the tactical approach that's becoming increasingly popular because it blends the best of both worlds: the individual focus of man-marking and the structural stability of zonal marking.

What is a Hybrid Marking System?

Think of it as a dynamic dance between man and zone. In a hybrid system, defenders primarily focus on defending zones but are ready to switch to man-marking when specific situations arise. It's a flexible approach that requires tactical awareness, communication, and the ability to adapt to the flow of the game.

How Does It Work?

Here's a breakdown of how hybrid marking systems typically operate:

1. **Zonal Foundation:** The defense sets up in a zonal structure, with each player responsible for a designated area of the pitch. This ensures a solid defensive shape and makes it harder for opponents to find gaps.
2. **Man-Marking Triggers:** Certain triggers prompt defenders to switch to man-marking. These triggers could be:
   - **Key Players:** A dangerous opponent receives the ball in a threatening position.
   - **Set Pieces:** Specific players are assigned to mark opponents on corners or free kicks.
   - **Tactical Instructions:** The coach might instruct a defender to man-mark a particular player for a certain period.
3. **Seamless Transition:** The switch between zonal and man-marking should be smooth and seamless. Defenders need to communicate effectively to ensure there are no overlaps or gaps in coverage.
4. **Return to Zone:** Once the trigger is no longer present, defenders return to their zonal responsibilities, maintaining the team's defensive shape.

Advantages of Hybrid Marking Systems:

- **Flexibility:** Hybrid systems offer the best of both worlds, allowing you to adapt to different game situations and opponent strategies.
- **Tactical Surprise:** The ability to switch between marking systems can catch opponents off guard and disrupt their attacking flow.

- **Targeted Defense:** You can neutralize specific threats by man-marking key players while maintaining a solid zonal structure for the rest of the defense.
- **Reduced Fatigue:** Defenders don't have to constantly chase opponents around the field, conserving energy for other aspects of the game.

Disadvantages of Hybrid Marking Systems:

- **Requires High Tactical Awareness:** Defenders need to be able to quickly recognize triggers and seamlessly transition between marking systems.
- **Communication is Key:** Clear and constant communication between defenders is essential to avoid confusion and maintain a cohesive defensive unit.
- **Potential for Mismatches:** If the wrong player is assigned to man-mark an opponent, it can create a mismatch and lead to defensive vulnerabilities.
- **Training and Practice:** Hybrid marking systems require extensive training and practice to master. Defenders need to develop the tactical awareness and communication skills necessary to execute the system effectively.

Implementing a Hybrid Marking System

If you're considering implementing a hybrid system, here are some key steps:

1. **Education:** Ensure all players understand the principles of both zonal and man-marking.
2. **Clear Triggers:** Define clear triggers for when defenders should switch to man-marking.
3. **Practice:** Dedicate training sessions to practicing the transition between zonal and man-marking.
4. **Communication:** Emphasize the importance of communication between defenders to maintain a cohesive unit.
5. **Adaptability:** Be prepared to adjust the system based on the game situation and the opponent's tactics.

Hybrid marking systems are not a one-size-fits-all solution. But when implemented effectively, they can provide a versatile and adaptable defensive approach that can give your team a significant advantage on the pitch.

CHAPTER 22: PLAYER MOVEMENTS AND ROTATIONS

Rotational Play in Midfield

This is where the real tactical ballet happens, with midfielders constantly shifting positions to create overloads, exploit spaces, and keep the opposition guessing.

It's Not Just About Passing

Rotational play isn't just about passing the ball around. It's about coordinated movement off the ball. Midfielders need to understand when to drop deep, when to push forward, when to drift wide, and when to occupy central spaces.

The Benefits of Rotation

Why bother with all this movement? Here's why:

- **Confuse the Defense:** By constantly shifting positions, midfielders make it difficult for opponents to track them and maintain a tight marking scheme.
- **Create Overloads:** Rotations can create numerical advantages in specific areas of the field, allowing your team to dominate possession and dictate the tempo.
- **Open Passing Lanes:** As midfielders move, they create new passing options and angles, making it harder for the opposition to intercept the ball.
- **Exploit Space:** Rotational play can open up spaces behind the opposition's midfield, allowing your team to penetrate their defense.

Types of Rotations

There are countless variations of rotational play, but here are a few common examples:

- **The Box Rotation:** Two central midfielders and two attacking midfielders constantly switch positions, forming a box-like shape.
- **The Pivot and Shuttlers:** One deep-lying midfielder (the pivot) stays back to provide defensive cover while two other midfielders (the shuttlers) move forward to join the attack.
- **The False 9 Rotation:** The striker drops deep to create space for midfielders to run into, while the attacking midfielders push forward into the vacated space.

Coordination is Key

Rotational play isn't just about individual movement; it's about team coordination. Midfielders need to understand each other's movements and anticipate their teammates' intentions.

The Coach's Role

The coach plays a crucial role in designing and implementing rotational play. They need to choose the right system for their players' strengths and weaknesses, train them on the specific movements, and communicate clear instructions during the game.

Positional Interchange in Attack

This is where your forward line becomes a shape-shifting puzzle, constantly switching roles and positions to unlock defenses and create scoring chances.

It's More Than Just Swapping Spots

Positional interchange isn't just about players randomly switching places. It's a choreographed dance, with each movement designed to exploit the opponent's weaknesses and create overloads in key areas.

The Benefits of Interchange

Why bother with all this movement? Here's why:

- **Unpredictability:** By constantly interchanging positions, attackers become difficult to mark and track. Defenders can't get comfortable, leading to confusion and gaps.
- **Creating Overloads:** Interchanges can create numerical advantages in specific areas of the pitch, overwhelming the defense and opening up passing lanes.
- **Exploiting Space:** As attackers move, they can drag defenders out of position, creating space for teammates to exploit.
- **Breaking Defensive Lines:** By switching positions, attackers can find pockets of space between the lines, making them available for through balls and creating scoring opportunities.

Examples of Positional Interchange

Let's look at a couple of common scenarios:

- **The Winger Cuts Inside:** The winger drifts into a central position, dragging their marker with them and opening up space for an overlapping full-back.
- **The Striker Drops Deep:** The striker moves into midfield to receive the ball, drawing a center-back out of position and creating space for an attacking midfielder to run in behind.
- **The False 9:** The striker drops deep and wide, acting as a playmaker and creating confusion in the defense.

Coordination and Communication

Successful positional interchange requires excellent communication and understanding between players. They need to anticipate each other's movements and make decisions based on the overall tactical plan.

The Coach's Role

The coach plays a crucial role in designing and implementing positional interchange. They need to choose a system that suits their players' strengths, train them on the specific movements, and communicate clear instructions during the game.

Positional interchange can be a game-changer when executed well. It adds a layer of unpredictability to your attack, making it difficult for opponents to defend and opening up a world of creative possibilities.

Defenders Joining the Attack

This isn't just about hoofing the ball upfield; it's a calculated tactic that can add an extra dimension to your offensive play and catch opponents off guard.

The Overlapping Run: A Classic Tactic

The most common way defenders join the attack is through overlapping runs. This is when a full-back surges forward past their winger, creating a 2v1 situation and forcing the defense to make a difficult decision.

Benefits of Overlapping Runs:

- **Stretching the Defense:** Overlapping runs widen the field, pulling defenders out of position and creating space for your attackers in central areas.
- **Creating Numerical Superiority:** The extra player in attack can overload the defense, making it harder for them to contain your team.
- **Surprise Element:** Defenders often focus on marking forwards and wingers, leaving overlapping full-backs unmarked and with space to deliver crosses or take shots.

Other Ways Defenders Can Contribute to the Attack:

- **Underlapping Runs:** Instead of going wide, the full-back cuts inside, offering a passing option in the half-space and creating a different angle of attack.
- **Playing Out from the Back:** Center-backs can initiate attacks by dribbling forward or playing accurate passes into midfield.
- **Joining the Attack in Set Pieces:** During corners or free kicks, tall defenders can become aerial threats in the opponent's box.
- **Long Throws:** A defender with a powerful throw-in can launch the ball into the penalty area, creating chaos and potential scoring chances.

Balancing Risk and Reward:

While defenders joining the attack can be highly effective, it's important to maintain defensive balance.

- **Covering the Space:** If a full-back pushes forward, a midfielder or another defender must be ready to cover the space they leave behind.
- **Communication:** Defenders need to communicate clearly with their teammates to ensure everyone is aware of their movements and tactical intentions.
- **Timing:** The timing of overlapping runs is crucial. They should be made at the right moment to catch the defense off balance and create the maximum impact.

Incorporating defenders into your attack adds a layer of unpredictability and can open up new avenues for creating scoring opportunities. However, it requires careful planning, coordination, and a willingness to take calculated risks.

CHAPTER 23: EFFECTIVE USE OF SUBSTITUTIONS AND IN-GAME CHANGES

Timing of Substitutions

Let's talk about the timing of substitutions in soccer. It's not just about who you bring on, but when you do it. Timing can be the difference between a game-changing substitution and one that falls flat.

The Golden Rule: Be Proactive, Not Reactive

Don't wait until your team is desperate or a player is injured. Use substitutions as a tactical weapon to gain an advantage before the opponent has a chance to react.

Key Moments for Substitutions:

- **Early in the Game (15-30 minutes):** If your starting lineup isn't clicking or you're being outplayed in a specific area, an early substitution can change the dynamic of the match.
- **Around Halftime (45-60 minutes):** Halftime is a natural break to assess the game and make adjustments. Introduce a fresh player to inject energy or change the tactical approach.
- **The Final Third (60-75 minutes):** This is when fatigue sets in and games often open up. A substitute with fresh legs and new ideas can exploit tired defenses.
- **Late in the Game (75+ minutes):** Depending on the scoreline, late substitutions can be used to chase a goal, protect a lead, or kill time.

Factors to Consider:

- **Scoreline:** Are you winning, losing, or drawing? This will heavily influence your substitution decisions.
- **Opponent's Tactics:** How is the opponent playing? Do they have any weaknesses you can exploit with a substitution?
- **Player Fatigue:** Are your players tiring? Fresh legs can make a huge difference, especially late in the game.
- **Tactical Flexibility:** Do you have substitutes who can offer different options and adapt to changing game situations?

The Psychological Impact:

Substitutions can also have a psychological effect on both teams. A well-timed substitution can lift your team's spirits and put doubt in the opponent's minds.

The Art of Timing:

The perfect timing for a substitution is often a gut feeling, a sense that now is the right moment to make a change. But by understanding the key moments and factors involved, you can make more informed decisions and maximize the impact of your substitutions.

Substitutions aren't just about replacing tired players; they're a tactical tool that can change the game in your favor. Use them wisely, and you can swing the momentum and exploit weaknesses.

Tactical Shifts

This is where in-game adjustments go beyond individual player changes and dive into transforming your team's entire approach.

The Chameleon Effect: Adapting to the Game

Think of your tactics like a chameleon blending into its surroundings. The game changes, and so should you. Tactical shifts aren't a sign of weakness; they show your ability to read the game and react effectively.

Triggers for a Tactical Shift:

- **The Scoreline:** If you're chasing the game, you might shift to a more attacking formation. If you're protecting a lead, you might opt for a more defensive setup.
- **Opponent's Weakness:** If you spot a vulnerability in their defense, adjust your tactics to exploit it. For example, if their fullbacks are often out of position, switch to a formation with wingers to attack the flanks.
- **Opponent's Change:** If the other team changes their tactics, you need to respond. Don't let them gain the upper hand by adapting to your initial plan.
- **Lack of Effectiveness:** If your current tactics aren't yielding results, don't be afraid to try something new. A change in formation or approach can inject new life into your team.

Common Tactical Shifts:

- **Formation Changes:** Switching from a 4-3-3 to a 3-5-2 can provide more defensive solidity or create overloads in midfield.
- **Attacking Style:** Shifting from a possession-based approach to a direct style can catch the opposition off guard and create scoring opportunities.
- **Defensive Approach:** Switching from zonal marking to man-marking can help you neutralize a specific threat.
- **Tempo:** Changing the tempo of the game can disrupt the opponent's rhythm. Speeding up the play can create chaos, while slowing it down can frustrate them.

Communication is Key

When making tactical shifts, clear communication is essential. Ensure your players understand the new plan, their individual roles, and the overall objective. Use hand signals, verbal cues, or even a whiteboard during breaks to clarify your instructions.

Practice Makes Perfect

Tactical shifts aren't something you can just wing on game day. Practice them in training so your players are familiar with different formations and systems.

CHAPTER 24: TACTICS FOR WEAKER TEAMS VS. TACTICS FOR STRONGER TEAMS

Strategies for Underdogs

It's not just about parking the bus; it's about being smart, organized, and exploiting the overconfidence of your stronger opponent.

Defense First, But Not Only

When facing a superior team, defensive solidity is paramount. But that doesn't mean you just bunker down and pray for a draw. You need a proactive defense that disrupts their rhythm and frustrates their attacks.

- **Deep Block:** Drop deep and compact the space between your lines. Make it difficult for them to penetrate your defense and force them to resort to long shots or crosses.
- **Disciplined Marking:** Stay tight to your assigned players and deny them space to turn and create. Don't get dragged out of position chasing the ball.
- **Tactical Fouls:** Sometimes, a well-timed tactical foul can break up a dangerous attack or prevent a counter-attack. Use them sparingly, though, as they can lead to cards and free kicks.

Slowing the Pace: Less is More

A slower pace favors the underdog. It limits the number of attacking opportunities for the stronger team and gives you more time to recover and regroup.

- **Possession Play:** When you have the ball, don't rush your passes. Keep it simple, circulate it around, and wait for the right moment to launch an attack.
- **Goal Kicks and Free Kicks:** Take your time with goal kicks and free kicks. It's a chance to catch your breath and reorganize your defense.
- **Time Wasting:** In the closing stages, if you're ahead or level, don't be afraid to milk every second. Slow down throw-ins, take your time with substitutions, and make the most of any stoppages in play.

Exploiting Their Overconfidence

Stronger teams often underestimate underdogs. Use that to your advantage.

- **Counter-Attacks:** Absorb their pressure and look for opportunities to hit them on the break. A quick transition and a well-placed pass can catch them off guard.
- **Set Pieces:** Corners, free kicks, and even throw-ins can be your best friend. Practice your routines and look to exploit any weaknesses in their set-piece defense.

The Mental Game

Being an underdog is as much a mental challenge as it is a tactical one. Stay focused, maintain your discipline, and don't get discouraged by early setbacks. Remember, you have nothing to lose and everything to gain.

Approaches for Dominant Teams

It's not just about having the best players; it's about using your superior skills and resources to control the game and impose your will on the opponent.

Dominating Possession: The Conductor's Baton

For dominant teams, possession is often the key to success. It allows you to dictate the tempo, wear down the opponent, and create a multitude of scoring chances.

- **Patient Build-Up:** Don't necessarily rush your attacks. Build from the back, circulate the ball, and wait for gaps to appear in the defense. Utilize short, sharp passes and intelligent movement to create triangles and diamonds that open up space.
- **Midfield Control:** Your midfielders are the heartbeat of your possession game. They should dictate the tempo, recycle possession, and initiate attacks.
- **Width and Depth:** Stretch the opponent's defense by utilizing the full width of the field. Full-backs should push high and wingers should hug the touchline.
- **Overloads:** Create numerical advantages in specific areas of the field by overloading one side or flooding the central zone. This will force the defense to react and open up spaces elsewhere.

Playing Fast: The Accelerator Pedal

While possession is crucial, dominant teams also need to know when to shift gears and play with speed. A quick transition from defense to attack can catch the opposition off balance and create high-quality scoring chances.

- **Counter-Pressing:** Win the ball back quickly after losing it. High-pressing forces the opponent to make mistakes and gives you the opportunity to launch a quick counter-attack.
- **Direct Passing:** Don't be afraid to play direct passes when the opportunity arises. A well-timed through ball can bypass the entire defense and put your attacker in on goal.
- **One-Two Combinations:** Quick one-two passes between players can unlock tight defenses and create space for shots.
- **Early Crosses:** If your opponent's defense is deep and compact, consider early crosses into the box to catch them off guard.

Versatility: The Multi-Tool

Dominant teams should be versatile in their approach. They should be able to adapt to different opponents and game situations.

- **Adapting to the Score:** If you're ahead, you can afford to be more patient and control possession. If you're behind, you might need to take more risks and play with more urgency.
- **Adjusting to the Opponent:** If your opponent sits deep and defends in numbers, you might need to be more patient and creative in your build-up play. If they press high, you might need to play more direct and exploit the space behind their defense.

Maintaining Balance: The Tightrope Walk

Dominant teams need to find the right balance between offense and defense.

- **Offensive Mindset:** Don't be afraid to attack. You have the players and the quality to create numerous scoring chances.
- **Defensive Responsibility:** Even dominant teams need to defend well. Maintain your defensive shape, track runners, and win duels.
- **Transitions:** Be prepared for quick transitions between defense and attack. This is where you can catch the opponent off guard and punish them.

The Mental Edge: The Winning Attitude

Being a dominant team isn't just about tactics and technique. It's also about having the right mentality.

- **Confidence:** Believe in your ability to dominate the game.
- **Aggression:** Play with intensity and purpose.
- **Ruthlessness:** When you create chances, take them. Don't let your opponent off the hook.

- **Resilience:** If you concede a goal, don't panic. Keep your composure and continue to play your game.

Dominant teams set the tone of the match. They take the initiative, control the game, and create a sense of inevitability. By mastering the principles discussed here and adapting them to your team's strengths and weaknesses, you can become a truly dominant force on the soccer field.

CHAPTER 25: GAME MANAGEMENT TACTICS

Playing from Different Scorelines (Winning, Losing, Drawing)

This is what we call game management, and it's a critical aspect of soccer tactics. The way you play when winning, losing, or drawing can be the difference between victory and defeat.

Winning: Protecting the Lead

You're ahead, but the game's not over. It's tempting to keep attacking, but a smart team knows how to protect their lead.

- **Defensive Shape:** Drop deeper, maintain a compact shape, and close down spaces. Make it difficult for the opponent to penetrate your defense.
- **Possession Play:** Keep the ball. The more you have it, the less the opponent can attack. Slow down the tempo and frustrate them.
- **Counter-Attacks:** Look for opportunities to hit them on the break. A quick transition can punish them for overcommitting.
- **Tactical Fouls:** A well-timed foul (not a reckless one!) can break up a dangerous attack and give your team a breather.

Losing: Chasing the Game

You're behind, and the clock's ticking. It's time to take risks and go for it.

- **Push Numbers Forward:** Send more players into attack, including full-backs and defensive midfielders.
- **Play Direct:** Forget the patient build-up. Pump long balls into the box, look for set pieces, and create chaos in the opponent's penalty area.
- **Take More Shots:** Don't be afraid to shoot from distance or take low-percentage chances. You need goals, and sometimes you have to gamble.
- **High Press:** Press high up the pitch to force turnovers and win the ball in dangerous areas.

Drawing: The Delicate Balance

A draw can be a good result, but it can also be frustrating. Your approach will depend on your overall objectives and the flow of the game.

- **Assess the Situation:** Are you happy with a draw, or do you need a win? Is your team dominating the game, or are you struggling to create chances?

- **Calculated Risks:** If you need a win, you'll need to take some risks, but don't throw caution completely to the wind.
- **Game Management:** If you're happy with a draw, focus on maintaining your defensive shape and frustrating the opponent. Look for opportunities to counter-attack, but don't overcommit.

Game management is about adapting to the situation and making smart decisions. By understanding how to play from different scorelines, you can maximize your chances of winning, minimize your chances of losing, and ultimately, achieve your goals.

Tactical Adjustments Based on Score

This is the art of game management, a critical skill for any soccer team.

Winning: Protecting Your Advantage

If you're ahead, don't get complacent. Shift your focus to defending the lead:

- **Drop Deeper:** Instead of pushing high, your team should retreat and compact the space between the lines, making it harder for the opponent to find gaps.
- **Keep Possession:** The ball is your friend. The more you have it, the less the opponent can attack. Slow down the tempo and frustrate them.
- **Look for Counters:** A quick transition can catch the opponent off guard as they push forward to equalize.
- **Tactical Fouls (with Caution):** A well-timed foul (not a reckless one!) can break up a dangerous attack, but be careful not to over-use this tactic.

Losing: Chasing the Game

If you're behind, it's time to take risks and increase the pressure:

- **Push Players Forward:** Send more players into attack, including full-backs and defensive midfielders.
- **Play More Direct:** Forget the patient build-up. Aim for long balls into the box, look for set pieces, and create chaos in the opponent's penalty area.
- **Take More Shots:** Don't be afraid to shoot from distance or take low-percentage chances. You need goals, and sometimes you have to gamble.
- **High Press:** Press high up the pitch to force turnovers and win the ball in dangerous areas. This can put the opponent under immense pressure.

Drawing: Balancing Act

A draw can be a positive outcome, but it can also be frustrating. Your approach depends on your goals and how the game is unfolding:

- **Analyze the Situation:** Are you content with a draw, or do you need a win? Is your team dominating the game, or struggling to create chances?
- **Calculated Risks:** If you need a win, take some risks, but don't go all-out attack and leave yourself vulnerable.
- **Game Management:** If you're happy with a draw, focus on maintaining your defensive shape and frustrating the opponent. Look for counter-attacking opportunities, but don't overcommit.

Protecting a Lead vs. Chasing a Game

Let's look into the contrasting tactics of protecting a lead versus chasing a game in soccer. It's a balancing act, shifting gears to match the situation and secure the desired outcome.

Protecting a Lead: The Art of Defense

When you're ahead, the game plan shifts from scoring goals to denying them. It's about maintaining composure, discipline, and a solid defensive structure.

- **Drop Deeper:** Instead of pressing high, your team retreats, forming a compact block that's harder to penetrate. This forces the opponent to resort to long-range efforts or hopeful crosses.
- **Possession is Key:** Keep the ball away from the opposition. The more time you spend in possession, the less time they have to attack. Slow down the tempo, frustrate their efforts, and let them chase shadows.
- **Counter-Attack Opportunities:** Look for chances to hit them on the break. As they push forward in search of an equalizer, gaps will appear in their defense, ripe for exploitation.
- **Tactical Fouls (with Caution):** A well-timed foul can disrupt a dangerous attack and give your team a breather. However, use this tactic sparingly and strategically, as accumulating cards can be detrimental.

Chasing a Game: The Offensive Surge

When you're behind, it's time to unleash the attacking hounds. This means taking risks, pushing numbers forward, and creating chaos in the opponent's penalty area.

- **Forward Surge:** Send more players into attack, including full-backs and defensive midfielders. Overload their defense and create numerical superiority in the final third.

- **Direct Approach:** Forget the patient build-up. Launch long balls into the box, look for set pieces, and aim for quick shots on goal. The priority is to get the ball in the net as quickly as possible.
- **Shoot on Sight:** Don't be afraid to test the goalkeeper from distance or take low-percentage chances. The more shots you take, the higher the probability of scoring.
- **High Press:** Press high up the pitch to force turnovers and win the ball in dangerous areas. This can put immense pressure on the opponent and lead to mistakes.

Use of Time-Wasting Tactics

Let's talk about the controversial yet effective world of time-wasting tactics in soccer. When used strategically, they can be a valuable tool in your game management arsenal, but it's a delicate balance between clever play and unsportsmanlike conduct.

When to Consider Time-Wasting

Firstly, time-wasting isn't always appropriate. It's most effective when you're in the lead, particularly in the latter stages of a match. The goal is to protect your advantage and see out the win, not to frustrate your opponents needlessly.

Mastering the Art of Time-Wasting

Here are some subtle and not-so-subtle techniques to wind down the clock:

- **Goalkeeper Shenanigans:** Taking your sweet time with goal kicks, pretending to be injured after a save, or delaying the restart of play can all eat up precious seconds.
- **Substitutions:** Using all your allotted substitutions, especially late in the game, can disrupt the flow and momentum of the match.
- **Injury Feigning:** While frowned upon, some players resort to exaggerating injuries to pause the game and catch their breath. Use this tactic cautiously and sparingly, as it can backfire if the referee catches on.
- **Ball Out of Play:** If the ball goes out of play, don't rush to retrieve it. Take your time, and if you're the throw-in taker, make sure you're properly set before launching the ball.
- **Slow Down the Tempo:** When in possession, focus on short passes and keeping the ball moving. Avoid risky plays that could lead to turnovers.

The Ethical Dilemma

Time-wasting walks a fine line between smart play and gamesmanship. It's important to be respectful of the game, the opponent, and the fans. Don't overuse these tactics, and avoid anything that could be considered unsportsmanlike.

Countering Time-Wasting:

If you're on the receiving end of time-wasting tactics, don't let it frustrate you. Stay focused on the game, press high to try and win the ball back quickly, and take advantage of any set-piece opportunities.

Mentality and Motivation in Different Game States

The scoreline, time remaining, and overall momentum can drastically shift your team's mentality and motivation.

Winning: The Confidence Trap

You're ahead, but the game isn't won. Don't let complacency creep in. Maintain focus and discipline. Avoid unnecessary risks, but don't completely abandon your attacking instincts. Look for opportunities to counter-attack and extend your lead, but also be prepared to defend resolutely.

Losing: The Urgency Factor

You're behind, and time is running out. Don't panic, but do increase the urgency. Be more direct in your play, take more risks, and push more players forward. Encourage your team to take shots from distance and be aggressive in their challenges. Remember, a single goal can change everything.

Drawing: The Tightrope Walk

A draw can be a positive result, but it can also feel like a missed opportunity. The key is to maintain focus and composure. Don't get reckless chasing a win, but also don't sit back and settle for a draw if you're capable of more. Look for opportunities to break the deadlock, but also be mindful of the opponent's counter-attacking threat.

The Importance of Adaptability

Game states can change quickly in soccer. A goal, a red card, or a shift in momentum can completely alter the dynamics of the match. Successful teams are adaptable, able to adjust their mentality and approach based on the current situation.

The Coach's Role

The coach plays a crucial role in managing the team's mentality. They need to keep players motivated and focused, regardless of the scoreline. They also need to be decisive in their tactical adjustments and communicate their game plan clearly.

The Power of Belief

No matter the scoreline, never give up. The belief that you can win, even when facing adversity, can be a powerful motivator. Encourage your teammates, stay positive, and keep fighting until the final whistle.

CHAPTER 26: TACTICAL LESSONS FROM THE WORLD'S BEST CLUBS

Case Studies: Barcelona, Bayern Munich, Manchester City

These teams have consistently showcased innovative and effective tactics that have revolutionized the way the game is played.

Barcelona: Tiki-Taka and Positional Play

Under Pep Guardiola's guidance, Barcelona perfected the art of tiki-taka, a possession-based style characterized by short, quick passes and constant movement. This approach suffocated opponents, limited their chances, and created numerous scoring opportunities.

Key takeaways from Barcelona's tiki-taka:

- **Patient Build-Up:** Barcelona prioritized patient build-up play from the back, using triangles and diamonds to maintain possession and probe for openings in the defense.
- **Quick Passing and Movement:** Players constantly moved into space, offering passing options and creating overloads in different areas of the field.
- **High Pressing:** When possession was lost, Barcelona immediately pressed high to regain the ball and launch another attack.
- **Positional Play:** Players were assigned specific zones on the pitch, ensuring a balanced structure and efficient movement both in and out of possession.

Bayern Munich: High Pressing and Wing Play

Bayern Munich, under coaches like Jupp Heynckes and Hansi Flick, have been known for their aggressive high pressing and devastating wing play.

Key takeaways from Bayern Munich's tactics:

- **High Pressing:** Bayern relentlessly pressed high up the pitch, forcing opponents into mistakes and winning the ball back in dangerous areas.
- **Wing Dominance:** They utilized the width of the field with overlapping full-backs and direct wingers who could deliver crosses or cut inside to shoot.

- **Counter-Attacking Threat:** Bayern's speed and precision in transition allowed them to punish opponents on the break.
- **Physicality and Intensity:** Their players were known for their physicality, winning aerial duels, and dominating midfield battles.

Manchester City: Total Football 2.0

Pep Guardiola's Manchester City has taken possession-based football to new heights, blending elements of tiki-taka with a more direct and vertical approach.

Key takeaways from Manchester City's tactics:

- **Positional Interchanges:** City's players constantly swap positions, making them difficult to mark and creating confusion for the defense.
- **False Nine:** They often deploy a false nine, a striker who drops deep to create space for attacking midfielders to exploit.
- **Full-Back Overloads:** City's full-backs push high and wide, creating overloads in wide areas and stretching the opponent's defense.
- **High Defensive Line:** They play with a high defensive line, compressing the space and forcing the opponent to play long balls.

Adaptability: The Common Thread

While each of these teams has its own unique style, they share a common thread: adaptability. They are not afraid to adjust their tactics based on the opponent, the game situation, or the scoreline.

- **Barcelona:** While known for tiki-taka, they were also capable of playing a more direct style when necessary.
- **Bayern Munich:** They could adjust their pressing intensity based on the opponent and the game state.
- **Manchester City:** While favoring possession, they were also lethal on the counter-attack.

Lessons Learned

By studying the tactics of these successful clubs, we can learn valuable lessons about:

- **The Importance of Possession:** Possession allows you to control the game, dictate the tempo, and create more scoring chances.
- **The Power of Pressing:** High pressing can disrupt the opponent's build-up play, force turnovers, and create goalscoring opportunities.

- **The Value of Movement:** Constant movement off the ball can create space, open up passing lanes, and confuse the defense.
- **The Need for Adaptability:** Successful teams are flexible and can adjust their tactics to suit different situations.

These are just a few examples of the tactical innovations these clubs have implemented. By studying their games, analyzing their strategies, and adapting their ideas to your own team's strengths and weaknesses, you can continue to evolve as a coach and elevate your team's performance.

Learning from Success

It's not just about copying what top clubs do; it's about understanding the principles behind their success and adapting them to your own team and context.

Principles, Not Just Plays

Don't get fixated on specific formations or set plays. Focus on the underlying principles that make these teams successful. Is it their relentless pressing? Their fluid positional play? Their quick transitions? By understanding the core principles, you can adapt them to your own team's strengths and weaknesses.

The Art of Adapting

Don't try to force a square peg into a round hole. What works for Barcelona might not work for your local amateur team. Consider your players' skill sets, your league's level of play, and the specific challenges you face. Adapt successful tactics to your unique context.

Analyze, Don't Just Watch

When you watch matches featuring top clubs, don't just be a passive observer. Actively analyze what's happening on the pitch. Why are they making certain decisions? How do they react to different situations? What patterns can you identify in their play?

Learn from Mistakes

Even the best teams make mistakes. Study their losses and near-misses. What went wrong? How did they get exposed? Learning from their failures can be just as valuable as learning from their successes.

Look Beyond the Top Clubs

Don't limit yourself to the biggest names in European football. Many successful teams around the world have developed unique and effective tactical approaches. Look for inspiration from teams in different leagues and countries.

The Importance of Continuous Learning

The world of soccer tactics is constantly evolving. New ideas and approaches emerge all the time. Stay curious, seek out new information, and never stop learning. Attend coaching courses, read tactical books, and engage with other coaches and analysts.

Adapting Strategies

Adapting strategies is a lesson straight from the playbook of top soccer clubs. It's not just about having a game plan; it's about evolving that plan in real time.

The Static Game Plan Myth

Forget the idea of a rigid, unchanging strategy. Soccer is dynamic, opponents adapt, and conditions shift. The best teams don't just have a Plan A; they have a Plan B, C, and D ready to go.

Reading the Game in Real Time

Pay close attention to what's happening on the pitch:

* **Opponent's Tactics:** Are they pressing high? Sitting deep? Focusing attacks down one flank?
* **Your Team's Performance:** Are your players executing the plan effectively? Are there any weaknesses being exposed?
* **Game State:** Are you winning, losing, or drawing? How much time is left?

The Halftime Reset

Halftime is a crucial opportunity to reassess and adjust. Analyze what's working, what's not, and how the opponent is reacting to your tactics. Don't be afraid to make bold changes if necessary.

In-Game Adjustments

Sometimes, you need to react on the fly. If your opponent surprises you with a tactical change, or if a key player gets injured, be prepared to adapt. This could involve switching formations, changing player roles, or altering your attacking approach.

The Coach's Role

The coach is the mastermind behind tactical adjustments. They need to be able to read the game, anticipate the opponent's moves, and make quick decisions. They also need to communicate their changes clearly to the players.

The Players' Role

Players need to be adaptable and intelligent on the field. They should be able to understand and execute the coach's instructions, even if it means changing their role or position mid-game.

Learning from the Best

Look at top clubs like Manchester City under Pep Guardiola. They're constantly tweaking their tactics, even within a single game. This flexibility allows them to stay one step ahead of their opponents and maintain control of the match.

Adapting strategies is a sign of a smart and well-prepared team. By being flexible and adaptable, you can turn the tide of a match, overcome adversity, and achieve victory.

APPENDIX

This appendix covers various formations, roles, and tactical concepts used in soccer.

4-4-2 Formation: A common soccer formation with four defenders, four midfielders, and two forwards.

4-3-3 Formation: A formation with four defenders, three midfielders, and three forwards, emphasizing attacking play.

4-2-3-1 Formation: A formation with four defenders, two defensive midfielders, three attacking midfielders, and one forward.

3-5-2 Formation: A formation with three defenders, five midfielders, and two forwards, often used to control the midfield.

5-3-2 Formation: A defensive formation with five defenders, three midfielders, and two forwards.

False Nine: A forward who drops deeper into the midfield to create space and confuse defenders.

High Press: A tactic where the team presses the opponent high up the pitch to regain possession quickly.

Low Block: A defensive strategy where the team defends deep in their own half to protect the goal.

Counter-Attack: A quick attacking move initiated after regaining possession, aiming to exploit the opponent's disorganization.

Tiki-Taka: A style of play characterized by short passing and movement, maintaining possession, and working the ball through various channels.

Man-Marking: A defensive strategy where each defender is responsible for marking a specific opponent.

Zone Defense: A defensive strategy where defenders cover specific areas of the pitch rather than marking individual opponents.

Sweeper: A central defender who plays behind the main line of defense to clear loose balls and cover for teammates.

Libero: Similar to a sweeper, a libero has more freedom to roam and contribute to both defense and attack.

Offside Trap: A defensive tactic where defenders move up the pitch together to catch an opponent offside.

Overlap: When a defender or midfielder runs past a teammate on the wing to receive the ball and create an attacking opportunity.

Underlap: When a player makes a run inside rather than outside a teammate on the wing.

Through Ball: A pass played between defenders for a teammate to run onto.

Switch of Play: Changing the point of attack by passing the ball to the opposite side of the pitch.

Width: Using the full width of the pitch to stretch the opponent's defense.

Depth: Utilizing both the length and width of the pitch to create space and passing options.

Compactness: Keeping players close together to reduce space for the opponent.

Pressing Traps: Setting up situations where opponents are deliberately lured into pressing areas where they can be surrounded and dispossessed.

Gegenpressing: A high-intensity pressing style aimed at winning the ball back immediately after losing it.

Possession Football: A style of play focused on maintaining possession of the ball to control the game.

Direct Football: A style of play focused on quickly moving the ball forward, often with long passes.

Target Man: A forward who holds up the ball and brings teammates into play.

Poacher: A forward who specializes in scoring goals from close range.

Box-to-Box Midfielder: A midfielder who contributes to both defense and attack, covering large areas of the pitch.

Deep-Lying Playmaker: A midfielder who dictates the play from a deeper position on the pitch.

Inverted Winger: A winger who plays on the opposite side of their stronger foot, allowing them to cut inside and shoot.

Wing-Back: A full-back with more offensive duties, often part of a formation with three central defenders.

Anchor Man: A defensive midfielder who protects the defense and breaks up opposition attacks.

Ball-Winning Midfielder: A midfielder who focuses on regaining possession through tackles and interceptions.

Shadow Striker: A forward who plays just behind the main striker, often dropping into midfield to link play.

Box-to-Box Midfielder: A versatile midfielder who contributes to both defense and attack, covering large areas of the pitch.

Deep-Lying Playmaker: A midfielder who dictates the play from a deeper position on the pitch.

Inverted Winger: A winger who plays on the opposite side of their stronger foot, allowing them to cut inside and shoot.

Wing-Back: A full-back with more offensive duties, often part of a formation with three central defenders.

Anchor Man: A defensive midfielder who protects the defense and breaks up opposition attacks.

Ball-Winning Midfielder: A midfielder who focuses on regaining possession through tackles and interceptions.

Shadow Striker: A forward who plays just behind the main striker, often dropping into midfield to link play.

False Full-Back: A full-back who moves into central midfield when in possession, adding an extra player in midfield.

Sweeper-Keeper: A goalkeeper who is comfortable playing outside the penalty area, often acting as an additional defender.

Double Pivot: Two central midfielders who sit in front of the defense, providing stability and linking play.

Central Winger: A player who drifts from the wing to the center of the pitch, often creating numerical superiority in midfield.

Diagonal Run: A run made at an angle to confuse defenders and create space.

Overlap: When a defender or midfielder runs past a teammate on the wing to receive the ball and create an attacking opportunity.

Underlap: When a player makes a run inside rather than outside a teammate on the wing.

Through Ball: A pass played between defenders for a teammate to run onto.

Switch of Play: Changing the point of attack by passing the ball to the opposite side of the pitch.

Width: Using the full width of the pitch to stretch the opponent's defense.

Depth: Utilizing both the length and width of the pitch to create space and passing options.

Compactness: Keeping players close together to reduce space for the opponent.

Pressing Traps: Setting up situations where opponents are deliberately lured into pressing areas where they can be surrounded and dispossessed.

Gegenpressing: A high-intensity pressing style aimed at winning the ball back immediately after losing it.

Possession Football: A style of play focused on maintaining possession of the ball to control the game.

Direct Football: A style of play focused on quickly moving the ball forward, often with long passes.

Target Man: A forward who holds up the ball and brings teammates into play.

Poacher: A forward who specializes in scoring goals from close range.

Box-to-Box Midfielder: A midfielder who contributes to both defense and attack, covering large areas of the pitch.

Deep-Lying Playmaker: A midfielder who dictates the play from a deeper position on the pitch.

Inverted Winger: A winger who plays on the opposite side of their stronger foot, allowing them to cut inside and shoot.

Wing-Back: A full-back with more offensive duties, often part of a formation with three central defenders.

Anchor Man: A defensive midfielder who protects the defense and breaks up opposition attacks.

Ball-Winning Midfielder: A midfielder who focuses on regaining possession through tackles and interceptions.

Shadow Striker: A forward who plays just behind the main striker, often dropping into midfield to link play.

False Full-Back: A full-back who moves into central midfield when in possession, adding an extra player in midfield.

Sweeper-Keeper: A goalkeeper who is comfortable playing outside the penalty area, often acting as an additional defender.

Double Pivot: Two central midfielders who sit in front of the defense, providing stability and linking play.

Central Winger: A player who drifts from the wing to the center of the pitch, often creating numerical superiority in midfield.

Diagonal Run: A run made at an angle to confuse defenders and create space.

AFTERWORD

From the evolution of classic formations to the cutting-edge tactics of today's game, we've covered a lot of ground in this book. But as with any aspect of soccer, the learning never stops.

The game is constantly evolving, and the tactics that seem innovative today may become outdated shortly. That's the beauty of soccer – it's a never-ending quest for excellence, a constant push to find new ways to outsmart your opponents and gain the all-important edge.

As you've learned throughout this book, modern soccer tactics are all about adaptability, fluidity, and a deep understanding of the game's nuances. It's not enough to simply memorize formations or follow a rigid playbook. The truly great players and coaches are those who can read the game, anticipate movements, and make quick decisions.

So, as you continue on your own tactical journey, whether as a player, coach, or simply a passionate fan, embrace the principles and concepts we've discussed, but don't be afraid to experiment, to innovate, and to challenge conventional wisdom.

The best tacticians are those who can blend tradition with innovation, who can find new ways to exploit weaknesses and create opportunities. They're the ones who can seamlessly transition from attack to defense and back again, who can maintain shape and balance while still taking calculated risks.

And above all, remember that tactics are a means to an end – the end being to play beautiful, exciting, and successful soccer. The formations, systems, and strategies we've explored are tools in your arsenal, but they should never overshadow the true essence of the game: skill, creativity, and the sheer joy of playing.

Study the greats, learn from their successes and failures, and never stop pushing the boundaries of what's possible on the pitch.

Who knows? Maybe one day, it will be your innovative tactics that redefine the modern game. And when that happens, we'll be here, ready to learn from you.

Made in the USA
Monee, IL
16 November 2024

093f1bc1-cd64-44a4-9398-e098d6f29621R01